THE SOCIAL AREAS OF LOS ANGELES

Analysis and Typology

THE SOCIAL AREAS
OF LOS ANGELES

Analysis and Typology

BY

ESHREF SHEVKY, 1893 –

AND

MARILYN WILLIAMS

Published for the John Randolph Haynes and Dora Haynes Foundation

GREENWOOD PRESS, PUBLISHERS
WESTPORT, CONNECTICUT

The Library of Congress has catalogued this publication as follows:

Library of Congress Cataloging in Publication Data

Shevky, Eshref.
 The social areas of Los Angeles.

 "Published for the John Randolph Haynes and Dora
Haynes Foundation."
 Bibliography: p. 163-166,
 1. Los Angeles--Social conditions. I. Williams,
Marilyn, 1921-   joint author. II. Title.
[HN80.L7S5 1972]   309.1'794'94   72-138180
 ISBN 0-8371-5637-8

THE JOHN RANDOLPH HAYNES AND DORA HAYNES FOUNDATION

◇　◇　◇

This report was prepared by the John Randolph Haynes and Dora Haynes Foundation. The interpretation of the data presented and the judgments which have resulted from the investigations made are primarily the views of the authors rather than of the Foundation. As a charitable and educational trust organized "for the purpose of promoting the well-being of mankind" the Foundation has no economic or social program of its own to promote.

Preface

Of all the large metropolitan centers of the country, Los Angeles is the least studied sociologically. There are scattered local studies, but these are disconnected investigations not directed toward questions of general significance. The particularized explanations that they yield do not enable us to ask relevant questions about the kind of urban society in which we live.

The present work is an attempt to establish the basis for developing a comprehensive knowledge of Los Angeles. In this first volume, some of the characteristics of urban society in California are examined against the background of social trends in the country as a whole. Within this framework, a method of analysis of population data is developed to describe the uniformities and the broad regularities observed in the characteristics of urban populations. The specific analysis of the population characteristics of Los Angeles is then presented, and a typology of urban forms is developed.

In a second volume, to be published subsequently, the uses of an urban typology will be discussed in some detail and material tracing the social meaning of a variety of urban differentials will be presented.

ESHREF SHEVKY
MARILYN WILLIAMS

Acknowledgments

THE PRESENT VOLUME *is an outgrowth of work begun when Mr. Charles W. Eliot was Director of Research at the Foundation, and we are indebted to him for the encouragement he gave us in the exploratory phases of our undertaking.*

We are deeply appreciative of the generous support given by the Board of Trustees of the Haynes Foundation to the work throughout the several years of its development. We especially wish to thank Mr. Reginald D. Johnson, Trustee of the Foundation, who frequently advised with us and encouraged us with his keen personal interest in the problems involved in the study. We are particularly indebted to Miss Anne M. Mumford, Trustee and Executive Secretary of the Foundation, who gave us unsparingly of her time. Her insights into urban problems and her detailed background of knowledge of Los Angeles have guided us in every phase of our work.

Dr. Ralph Beals, Dr. Edwin A. Cottrell, and Dr. Gordon S. Watkins, as members of the Consultative Committee of the Foundation, reviewed the draft of the manuscript in the course of its preparation, and we profited from their counsel. Dr. Philip Neff of Pomona College, one of our colleagues on the staff of the Foundation, read the manuscript and made a number of helpful suggestions for revision.

In the final organization of the material we have greatly profited from discussions with members of the Pacific Coast Committee on Community and Area Studies of the Social Science Research Council. Dr. Leonard Bloom, Dr. William S. Robinson, Dr. Calvin F. Schmid, Dr. Robert C. Tryon, Dr. Paul Wallin, members of the Committee, have read the manuscript and made valuable suggestions.

To Dr. Leonard Bloom and Dr. Robert C. Tryon we owe a special debt of gratitude for the stimulation we have received from them in the solution of a number of problems of method.

Whatever level of excellence has been achieved in the development and presentation of our material is in no small measure due to the com-

petent and painstaking work of those who have been associated with us in the execution of our plan of study. Miss Lucile Murphy carried the burden of much of the computation and organization of statistical data and helped us in many other ways. Miss Olive Reeks assisted us in the later phases of the work. Miss Phyllis DiBenedetto and Miss Bessie Gerolamo have contributed their skill in the preparation of the manuscript for publication.

Special thanks are due to Mr. Paul Silvius, who helped us with the problems of design and execution of the graphic material. Mr. Howard R. Saunders has compiled the maps and prepared the final tracings of all the diagrams. The successful integration of the graphic material with the presentation in the text, which we hope has been accomplished, is chiefly due to his cartographic skill and painstaking workmanship.

E.S.
M.W.

Contents

TABLES

FIGURES

I. The City within the Framework of Social Trends

In AMERICAN SOCIOLOGY, the study of the city and the comparative study of cities represent two separate tendencies. Until very recently, American workers in the field have shown little interest in the comparative study of cities. They have tended to limit their inquiry to the contemporary American city, especially to the American city in its most spectacular metropolitan form. But here also there has been a startling lack of comparative knowledge. It is partly as a consequence of this situation that the brilliant formulations of Robert Park, which provided the original impetus for the detailed ecological studies of Chicago, ultimately resulted in the development of a non-experimental, descriptive method. The influence of this tradition in the study of the city still persists in research and teaching, but its organizing principles no longer appear congruent with the postulates and theories with which social scientists at present operate.

In the scientific study of society, attention has come to be focused more and more on structural problems, on problems of institutional organization and function, and on the interrelationships of these with human behavior. In the analysis of these problems, comparative knowledge has become indispensable.

Robert and Helen Lynd in their pioneer studies of Middletown,[1] and W. Lloyd Warner and his associates in their more elaborate researches reported in the Yankee City Series,[2] applied this comparative point of view to the study of the relatively small modern community.

When the Urbanism Committee of the National Resources Board undertook to prepare the first national survey of American cities,[3] its perspective was in the comparative tradition, and the ultimate frame of reference adopted was the institutional framework of the whole American society. Against this broad canvas the assimilation of immigrant groups, for example, which loomed so large as the focal point of urban studies a decade or so earlier, became a minor detail.

---

[1] *Middletown* (New York, 1929) and *Middletown in Transition* (New York, 1937).
[2] W. L. Warner and Paul S. Lunt, *The Social Life of a Modern Community* (1941) (Vol. I of the Yankee City Series), and subsequent volumes of the series (Yale University Press, 1942–1947).
[3] National Resources Committee, *Our Cities—Their Role in the National Economy* (Washington, D.C., 1937).

The study of the very large cities is at present impeded, not only because of the enormous practical difficulties to be overcome but also because of the many unsettled problems of method to guide research within the framework of a unified social science.[4] In the pages that follow, an effort is made to deal with some of the difficulties by utilizing certain objective criteria of urbanization and stratification in modern society as bases upon which to unify the study of the city with the comparative study of cities. We cannot understand the structure of cities without understanding the structure and function of urban society itself, and since urban society is the product of the movement of people it is necessary that we first establish the framework of trends within which that movement takes place. This we attempt to do in this initial chapter.

Every city is a product of its time and can only be understood in terms of the society in which it comes into being. This observation is supported by common sense and is justified by the judgment of those who have made comparative studies of cities. If we are to understand the social system as a whole, we have to visualize it as a complex whole, changing in time. To do this it is often necessary to deviate from the conventions of the departmentalized social sciences. As students of the city, we are as much interested in the technology that makes the city possible as we are in the pattern of custom and deliberate choice that shapes its outward form; we are as keenly interested in the distribution of prestige and power and in the distribution of income as we are in the age structure of the population and the changing function of the family. Perhaps none of these preoccupations are reflected adequately or meaningfully enough in our material. They have, however, guided our choices of what to look for, what trends to examine, and what measures to define and compute in order to reduce the complexity of the phenomena under observation.

THE CHANGING OCCUPATIONAL STRUCTURE

The manner in which the working population is distributed among the three main occupational groups is significantly related to the economic organization and the class system of each society. The relative proportions of the farmer, artisan, and trader groups remain constant at any given stage of economic development. When these proportions

---

[4] For a recent discussion of these unsettled problems of method, see August B. Hollingshead, "Community Research: Development and Present Condition," *American Sociological Review*, 13 (1948), pp. 136–146.

change, they do so in some definite manner in relation to the changes in the economic organization and the total social system.

In all modern countries, changes in the economic organization, with consequent alteration in social relations, have been accompanied by a movement of working population from agriculture to manufacture and from manufacture to commerce and services. This has been the mecha-

TABLE 1

DISTRIBUTION OF THE WORKING POPULATION IN THE UNITED STATES, 1820–1940

Year	Agriculture, forestry, fishing	Mining	Manufacture and building	Trade, transport, communication	Domestic, personal, professional
	per cent	per cent	per cent	per cent	per cent
1820................	72.3	0.2	12.1	2.5	12.8
1830................	70.8	0.3	13.3	3.1	12.5
1840................	68.8	0.3	14.6	3.8	12.3
1850................	64.8	1.2	16.4	5.4	12.2
1860................	60.2	1.6	18.3	7.4	12.4
1870................	53.8	1.4	21.2	10.4	13.1
1880................	49.4	1.5	24.0	12.2	12.8
1890................	42.6	1.7	25.6	15.7	14.4
1900................	37.4	2.0	27.0	18.7	14.8
1910................	31.9	2.6	28.4	21.3	15.8
1920................	26.7	2.6	30.6	25.0	15.0
1930................	22.5	2.4	29.3	24.6	21.2
1940................	18.4	2.2	29.5	29.0	21.0

SOURCE: Colin Clark, *Conditions of Economic Progress* (London, 1940), p. 185. Figures for 1940 added. Original data from P. K. Whelpton, "Occupational Groups in the United States, 1820–1920," *Journal of the American Statistical Association*, September, 1926, p. 339.

nism of the increasing productivity of the European system throughout the whole modern period, and was the basic instrument of social transformation over the continental United States in relatively recent times.

In occupation statistics the vast number of specific occupations for which information is available are brought together in major industry groups. Manufacturing and construction, agriculture, and wholesale and retail trade appear as the chief categories, in the order named, while transportation, communication and public utilities, finance, insurance and real estate, personal services and professional and related services, and government appear severally as of minor importance.

This classification of the working population, which is the one most commonly used, tends to obscure the importance of the one overwhelming fact which has characterized modern development, namely, the enormous growth in contemporary society of the managerial, clerical, and service functions. The characteristic shift has been from the occupations concerned with manual productive operations to the

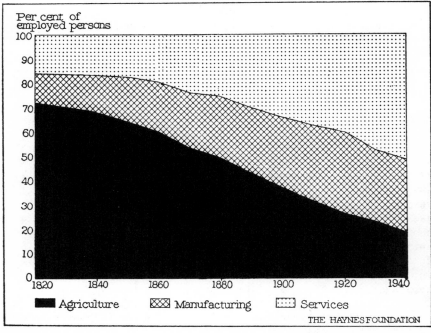

Fig. 1. Distribution of the working population in the United States, 1820–1940. Source: Colin Clark, *Conditions of Economic Progress* (London, 1940), p. 185. Figures for 1940 added. (Because of changes in classification in the 1940 census, the material for that year is only roughly comparable to that for other years. The percentage distribution for 1940, therefore, represents an approximation, and has been included to indicate the continuation of the trends.)

supervisory and clerical occupations. This tendency has been true not only in industrial production; it has influenced all other occupational levels as well. It would appear to be the tendency of modern industrial systems that production gains more in capital than in man power. The distributive and administrative machinery of the system absorbs a continually growing proportion of the number of employed persons.

The statistics of these changes in the United States during the last 120 years are shown in table 1 and figure 1. The details of the industrial classification given in table 1 are grouped in figure 1, according to their characteristics, as primary, secondary, and tertiary productive activity, but labeled, for convenience, agriculture, manufacturing, and services. Primary production includes agriculture, lumbering, and fishing; secondary production includes manufacturing, mining, building; services include trade, transportation, communication, and personal and professional services.

TABLE 2

DISTRIBUTION OF THE WORKING POPULATION IN CERTAIN COUNTRIES, 1930–1944

Country	Agriculture	Manufac- turing	Services
	per cent	per cent	per cent
Bulgaria...........................	67	17	15
India.............................	63	14	22
Poland............................	62	18	20
Spain.............................	57	24	18
Hungary...........................	54	25	22
Finland...........................	51	30	19
Italy.............................	43	31	26
Denmark...........................	36	28	37
Sweden............................	32	29	38
France............................	25	40	35
Germany...........................	24	39	37
Australia.........................	24	29	46
United States.....................	19	31	50
Great Britain.....................	7	43	50

SOURCE: Colin Clark, *Conditions of Economic Progress* (1940), p. 179.

As is shown in figure 1, the proportion of workers engaged in primary production has steadily declined in the United States from a little over 72 per cent in 1820 to approximately 18 per cent in 1940. The proportion in manufacturing, building, and mining rose to a maximum in 1920, declined by 1930, and was unchanged in 1940. The detailed examination of the changes in tertiary production shows that the proportion of workers in trade, transportation, and communication rose to a maximum in 1920, and has since declined, the surplus of workers in tertiary production being in large part absorbed in personal and professional services.

As Colin Clark has pointed out,[5] we can draw our conclusions with

[5] *Conditions of Economic Progress* (London, 1940), pp. 176–177.

TABLE 3

DISTRIBUTION OF THE WORKING POPULATION IN CERTAIN STATES, 1940

State	Agriculture	Manufac-turing	Services
	per cent	per cent	per cent
Mississippi	58	13	29
Arkansas	52	14	35
Alabama	40	24	36
Iowa	36	16	48
North Carolina	34	31	35
Montana	32	20	48
Virginia	25	28	48
Indiana	18	36	47
Washington	15	29	57
Michigan	12	43	45
California	11	24	65
Pennsylvania	6	44	49
New York	4	33	68
New Jersey	3	42	52

SOURCE: United States Census, 1940.

TABLE 4

DISTRIBUTION OF THE WORKING POPULATION IN CERTAIN CITIES, 1940

City	Agriculture	Manufac-turing	Services
	per cent	per cent	per cent
Pittsburgh	1	47	51
Cleveland	1	42	55
Cincinnati	1	39	55
New York	1	33	62
Los Angeles	3	27	68
San Francisco	2	23	75

SOURCE: United States Census, 1940.

respect to this trend either from an examination of the present situation in different parts of one country, or in different countries, or from examining figures for each country over a series of years. Tables 2, 3, and 4 describe the comparative situation in different countries and in the different parts of the United States.

In low-income, industrially less advanced countries, an overwhelming proportion of the working population is concentrated in primary production. With each succeeding step in industrial development, the population in secondary and tertiary production increases until levels observed in Great Britain, the United States, and Australia are achieved. The trend is the same when the different parts of a continental economy (for convenience, the different states in the United States) are compared with one another. Viewed against this background, the enormous expansion of trade and service occupations in California and in the Pacific Coast area is to be seen as part of a larger world pattern and as an extension of a persistent trend in the country as a whole.

THE DECLINING PROPORTION OF CHILDREN

Throughout the Occidental world a demographic transition has accompanied urbanization and the shift from a rural-familial to an urban-industrial economy. Starting with high fertility and mortality rates, the movement in all western countries has been toward a balance of births and deaths, less wasteful of life.

In some of the larger cities of western Europe in the eighteenth century, death rates as high as 50 per 1,000 were recorded. In these larger cities, deaths exceeded births by a very wide margin, and their growth was due solely to migration. The enormous growth of the European population as a whole and its expansion overseas became possible only when the basic alterations of productive activity and the introduction of public sanitation brought about a decline in the death rate.

There is no evidence to indicate that the growth of population in European countries in modern times was anywhere associated with any significant increase in the birth rate. On the contrary, all the evidence points to a continuous decline in the birth rate in all western countries during the entire period of modernization. The rapid urbanization of these countries became possible initially when trade and manufacturing could expand independently of agriculture. The changes in the mode of living of large numbers of persons which resulted from this shift were at the very center of the process of modernization with its ever-widening influence.[6]

Lowered fertility and the small-family pattern were important elements in the changes that were taking place, and they have since gone hand in hand with the rise of real income, the spread of education, and

[6] Kingsley Davis, "The World Demographic Transition," *Annals of the American Academy of Political and Social Science*, 237 (January, 1945), pp. 3-5.

the improvement of living conditions. In a recent study of European population, Dudley Kirk[7] describes the contemporary situation in the following terms:

The small family pattern is characteristically associated with superior education, better living conditions, and the urban social environment. The most highly developed areas, and especially the cities, are generally not replacing themselves. The most isolated and, in many respects, the poorest populations have the highest present and potential rates of growth. Fertility was lowest in the countries of northwestern and central Europe that have played a leading role in contemporary civilization, and progressively higher with increasing geographic and social distance from the urban heart of Europe.

In the United States, data on births and deaths are extremely fragmentary for the earlier years, and changes in the trend of the birth rate can only be traced with some difficulty. The birth-registration area was not established until 1915, and the uniform recording of births did not become a reality in all the states until 1933. In the absence of registration data for the earlier years, measures of fertility have been developed which rely on the age statistics of the successive censuses as far back as the year 1800. Walter F. Wilcox, who first analyzed these census data, found in the ratio of children under 5 years of age to 1,000 women 16 to 44 years of age the best indication of the trend of the birth rate for the entire period. In studying this material, Wilcox compared the changes in the birth rates of the United States during the nineteenth century with the changes in France during the same period,[8] France being a classic example of a country with a declining birth rate. He found the birth rate to be higher in the United States than in France, but its decrease in this country since 1800 he found to be almost as regular and much more rapid than its decline in France.

Subsequent to Wilcox's demonstration of this long-term trend, P. K. Whelpton[9] showed that there was a marked difference in different communities in the number of children per thousand women of childbearing ages as long ago as 1800. He classified the states as agricultural, semi-industrial, and industrial. He found that the ratios of children to women sharply declined as the degree of industrialization (and urbanization) increased.

[7] *Europe's Population in the Interwar Years* (League of Nations Publications, II, Economic and Financial, 1946, II A 8), p. 57.

[8] "The Change in the Proportion of Children in the United States and in the Birth Rate in France during the Nineteenth Century," American Statistical Association, *Publications*, 12 (1910–1911), pp. 490–499.

[9] "Industrial Development and Population Growth," *Social Forces*, 6 (1928), p. 462.

In a more recent study seeking to determine the possible existence of fertility differentials prior to large-scale industrial and urban development, A. J. Jaffe[10] discovered that early regional and class differences in fertility were as large as they are today and presumably had existed for a long time. According to Jaffe's findings, the states having the lowest "gross" reproductive rates in 1800 were those along the Atlantic seaboard, particularly in lower New England. In the Middle Atlantic States, the Carolinas, and upper New England the rates were

TABLE 5

NUMBER OF CHILDREN UNDER FIVE YEARS OF AGE PER THOUSAND WOMEN
SIXTEEN TO FORTY-FOUR YEARS OF AGE IN THE UNITED STATES, 1800–1940

Year	Number	Year	Number
1800.	1000	1880.	635
1810.	976	1890.	554
1820.	928	1900.	541
1830.	877	1910.	508
1840.	835	1920.	486
1850.	699	1930.	407
1860.	714	1940.	342
1870.	649		

SOURCE: Walter F. Wilcox, *Studies in American Demography* (Cornell University Press, 1940), table 118, p. 267, and Warren S. Thompson, *Population Problems* (New York, 1942), table 97, p. 251.

somewhat higher. The highest rates were in the most recently settled areas along the frontier stretching from the Lakes to the Gulf. The fertility differences discovered by Jaffe were too great in the beginning of the nineteenth century to have originated then, which leads to the suggestion that they had existed since the beginning of the eighteenth century or even perhaps reached back to an earlier period.

There is no doubt that the steady decline in fertility in the United States during the nineteenth century first became evident in the urban-industrial centers of lower New England, and that the rapid fall of the birth rate occurred elsewhere, spreading out from those centers in relation to the industrialization and urbanization of the country.

The existing regional and class differences in fertility are evidences of important differentials in the degree of urbanization in society—

[10] "Differential Fertility in the White Population in Early America," *Journal of Heredity*, 31 (1940), p. 408.

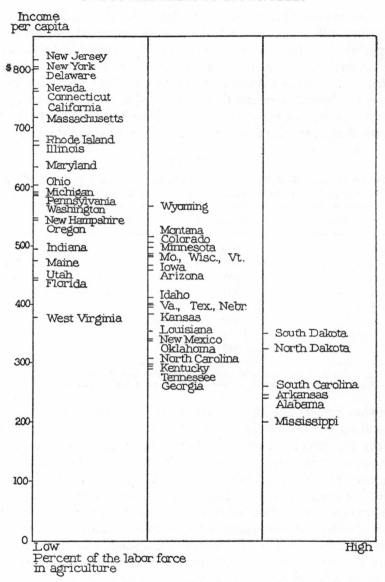

Fig. 2. Income per capita related to the percentage of the labor force in agriculture, 1939. Source: Louis H. Bean, "International Industrialization and Per Capita Income," in National Bureau of Economic Research, *Studies in Income and Wealth*, Vol. 8 (New York, 1946), table 2, p. 129.

In our presentation of this figure, the range of variation among the states for the percentage of the labor force in agriculture has been divided into three equal intervals. The lowest percentage is 2.1, in Rhode Island, and the highest is 59.0, in Mississippi. The limits of the three intervals are (in percentages): 2.1–20.7 (low); 20.8–39.3; 39.4–58.0 (high).

urbanization, not in a purely quantitative sense of numbers of people living in cities, but in the sense of basic differences in fundamental aspects of living. In this respect, urban society is still passing through a period of transition, and the declining proportion of children is an element in the changes that are taking place.

During the past several decades, the proportion of children to women of childbearing ages declined so precipitately that a straight-line extension of the trend pointed to the extraordinary result of no children at all in an immense population moving toward old age. The population movements since 1940 represent a sharp departure from this straight-line trend, but it is perhaps premature to look upon the recent large gains in the birth rate as indicating a permanent reversal of the long-term trend in the declining proportion of children.

THE CONTINENTAL PATTERN

The transfer of workers from agriculture to manufacture and trade was the necessary condition of rapid urbanization throughout the last one hundred years. Shifts in the character of economic opportunity brought about by increasing urbanization and industrialization caused changes in the regional distribution of workers. A complex occupational hierarchy developed, giving rise to differentials with ramifications in other social areas. As has just been pointed out above, one of the most far-reaching consequences of these social changes was the association of a declining birth rate with urbanization.

These deep-seated alterations in American society occurred at a different pace in different regions, sharpening the existing divergencies and growing into highly persistent regional contrasts. For the country as a whole the greatest differences are between the farm and the town populations. Regionally, differences in social organization are sharpest between regions that are predominantly urban-industrial and those that are predominantly rural.

If we examine the situation state by state, we find that the stage and the pattern of industrialization are major factors making for income differences in different parts of the country. Figure 2 traces the relation of per-capita income in various states to the proportion of working population engaged in agriculture.

One of the most significant indications of differences in regional development is supplied by the variations in the pattern of industrialization, that is, by the variations in the distribution of workers in the three main industrial groups, namely, agriculture, manufacture, and trade and services. If we follow the grouping of the states, on the basis of similarity of characteristics, in six regions as suggested by Odum,[11]

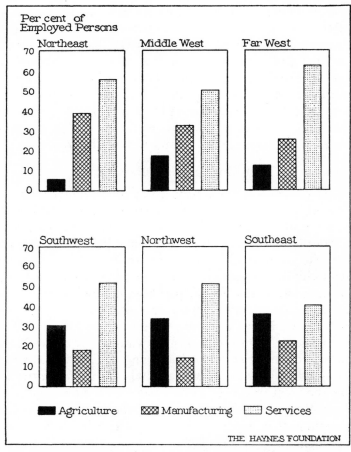

Fig. 3. Regional differences in the percentage of employed persons in three major industry groups, 1940. Source: *Statistical Abstract of the United States, 1944–1945*, table 146, pp. 150–151.

the form of distribution of workers in the three main industrial groups falls in two distinctive types. These are types associated with regions that are mainly rural and the regions that are mainly urban. (Fig. 3.)

With respect to major characteristics and the chief features of their

[11] In *Southern Regions of the United States*, by Howard W. Odum, for the Southern Regional Committee of the Social Science Research Council (Chapel Hill, 1936).

social organization, California and the entire Pacific Coast are more nearly like the urban-industrial northeastern section than any other region in the country. The three urban regions of the country, the Northeast, the Middle States, and the Far West, exhibit similar characteristics. Whatever index is chosen, the sharpest regional contrasts are between these urbanized regions and the rest of the country.

Regional differences in fertility.—Fertility differences between regions are associated with differences in the rate of urbanization and industrialization of different regions. The first major shift in the fertility of American population occurred in New England in the early 1800's. The decline spread westward in close association with the growth of cities and the industrialization of the country.

On the Pacific Coast, the decisive shift in the fertility of population occurred less than one hundred years ago. In 1860 the Pacific Coast was among regions of highest fertility in the nation (700–1,000 children under 5 per 1,000 women of childbearing age). By 1900 only the New England States, New York, and Ohio had as low a fertility as California (300–400 per 1,000 women of childbearing age). In 1940, fertility in the United States ranged from 242 for New York to 518 for New Mexico. California, with New Jersey, New York, Massachusetts, and Connecticut, was among the seven states having fertility ratios lower than 300. The position of the various regions with respect to fertility in 1940 was as follows:

Region	Children under 5 per 1,000 women 15–44
Northeast	280
Far West	285
Middle States	310
Southwest	380
Northwest	380
Southeast	400

Regional differences in age distribution.—If we divide the population into three groups, childhood, maturity, and older age, the mature population, those in the most productive ages (20–65) make up 55 per cent of the total population for the nation as a whole. Age distribution of the American population has been strongly influenced by foreign immigration, which accounts for this relatively large proportion of persons in the productive ages. Rural-urban shifts of population through the selective migration of persons in productive ages and the course of internal migration have the same general effect on age distribution in the industrial sections of the country and the western states. Thus, the highest percentage of mature-age groups is found in the northeastern states, 55.9 per cent, followed by the Far West, 55.5 per cent. Areas of out-migration show the smallest percentages: the Southeast, 53.3 per cent, and the Northwest with the smallest proportion of mature persons, 52.2 per cent.

In the distribution of children and older-age groups, contrasts are again between the areas of out-migration and the areas of in-migration, between the urban-industrial regions and the rural regions. States with older populations are in New England and the Far West, followed by the Middle States. With respect to the proportion of children below fourteen years of age the same group of states shows the smallest percentages. Thus, high-income regions, the Northeast, the Far West, and the Middle States, have the smallest proportion of children to the total population. Regions with relatively low income have the largest proportion. Children below fourteen years of age make up almost one-third of the total population in the Southeast, the region with lowest income.

Reverting once again to the observations of Colin Clark,[12] we note his fundamental generalization that modern economies tend to move toward more complex organizations and higher income levels in three steps: first, the intensification of primary production, agriculture, forestry, and mining; second, the expansion of manufacturing industries; third, the opening of tertiary pursuits to service the rest of the economy. Careful examination of available evidence suggests that we may well extend this generalization to include the broad regularities in population and social organization accompanying these changes in economic organization.

Here again, we can draw our conclusions with respect to these changes either from an examination of the present-day situation in different social areas, or by examining the course of events for each area over a series of years. When this is done, it is seen that the present-day characteristics of the population of California and of the entire Pacific Coast are not the sole peculiarities of these regions. They are characteristics generally associated with urban-industrial development, end products of orderly processes embracing the entire country.

[12] *Conditions of Economic Progress*, pp. 176–177.

Forms of social organization in urban-industrial and western areas would appear to be forms toward which other sections of the country tend to approximate as time goes on.

Urban character of California.—Adna Weber begins his book *The Growth of Cities in the Nineteenth Century* with a comparison of the distribution of population in the United States in 1790 with that in Australia in 1891.[13] Australia in 1891 had the same number of people as the America of 1790. It was peopled largely by men of the same European background, and it was still a new country, with undeveloped resources. But Australia was of the nineteenth century rather than the eighteenth, and that was the vital point which explained the striking difference in the distribution of population in the two countries at these two different periods. In 1790, of a population of about three million in the United States only 3 per cent lived in towns of ten thousand or more. In Australia in 1891, of a population of approximately the same size, fully 33 per cent lived in towns and cities of ten thousand or more.

To this comparison we may add the record of California as an illustrative example from the present century. In 1920, California had a population somewhat in excess of three million, had completed one cycle of its contemporary development, and was entering its present phase of growth. Even in 1920, California society was predominantly urban in character. More than 60 per cent of the population lived in towns and cities of ten thousand or more.

1790

Population of the United States. 3,929,214
Population of cities of 10,000 or more. 123,551
Proportion living in cities of 10,000 or more. . . . . 3.14 per cent

1891

Population of 7 colonies of Australia. 3,809,895
Population of cities of 10,000 or more. 1,264,283
Proportion living in cities of 10,000 or more. . . . . 33.2 per cent

1920

Population of California. 3,426,861
Population of cities of 10,000 or more. 2,128,910
Proportion living in cities of 10,000 or more. . . . . 62.1 per cent

---

[13] Adna Ferrin Weber, *The Growth of Cities in the Nineteenth Century—A Study in Statistics* (New York, 1899), p. 1.

The contemporary phase of development on the west coast of the United States started from a higher level of urbanization than obtained in any other section of the country at the time, except the North Atlantic States. This can be traced through the census reports and early becomes evident from the record. As early as 1870, California was among the ten most urban states in the country. In 1900, it was seventh in rank. Since then, the urbanization of California has kept pace with that of the most urban sections, as is shown in table 6.

TABLE 6

THE TEN MOST URBAN STATES IN 1870, 1900, AND 1940

(All percentages based on the 1940 definition. Figures for Rhode Island omitted.)

No.	1870		1900		1940	
	State	Per cent urban	State	Per cent urban	State	Per cent urban
1	Mass.	67	Mass.	86	Mass.	89
2	N.Y.	50	N.Y.	73	N.Y.	83
3	N.J.	44	N.J.	71	N.J.	82
4	Md.	38	Conn.	60	Ill.	74
5	Penn.	37	Penn.	55	Calif.	71
6	Calif.	37	Ill.	54	Conn.	68
7	Conn.	33	Calif.	52	Ohio	67
8	La.	28	Md.	50	Penn.	67
9	Ohio	26	Ohio	48	Mich.	66
10	Del.	25	Mich.	39	Md.	59

SOURCE: United States Census, 1940.

When gold was discovered in California in 1848, the industrial organization of the eastern United States was in the early phases of a new cycle of growth. This circumstance profoundly influenced the resource organization of the state and in large measure determined its urban character. California supplies perhaps one of the best examples of the principle that the opening of new countries does not provoke the upsweep of a long wave of economic development. On the contrary, growth cycles in already established economies make the exploitation of new countries, new markets, and new sources of raw materials necessary and possible.

It is for this reason that the American occupation of much of the southwestern land, after the Mexican War, had this characteristic in common: early occupation was not by settlers, but chiefly through the infiltration of traders, promoters, and professional men.

In California, free land, or cheap land, virtually never existed after the American occupation. The accumulation of vast quantities of land in advance of settlement was carried out with peculiar thoroughness. When, in the years following the discovery of gold, great expansion of agricultural activity took place, the essential frame of this development was the monopoly of land and water, and the production of one

TABLE 7

POPULATION OF METROPOLITAN DISTRICTS OF CALIFORNIA, 1940

District	Population
	millions
State..	6.90
Los Angeles.................................	2.90
San Francisco–Oakland......................	1.42
San Diego...................................	0.25
Sacramento..................................	0.15
San Jose....................................	0.12
Fresno......................................	0.10
Stockton....................................	0.08

SOURCE: United States Census, 1940.

speculative crop after another dominated economic activity. The character of the decade 1860–1870 was given by the large-scale growing of wheat; the high price of wool in the decade 1870–1880 stimulated a great increase in flocks of sheep. During the decade 1880–1890 the transition to the intensive cultivation of fruit took place. Subsequently, large-scale production of specialty crops has come to dominate California agriculture.

The relative size of the two great urban agglomerations, north and south, as compared with the rest of the urban centers, is a measure of the enormous urban concentration of California. Nearly three-fourths of the people of California live within the seven metropolitan districts, as is shown in table 7. The Los Angeles and San Francisco–Oakland areas together account for 62 per cent of the population. Forty-two per cent live within the Los Angeles metropolitan area alone. Recent estimates place the total population of the state at a figure in excess of ten millions and that of the county in excess of four millions. There are no comparable estimates of the increase in the size of metropolitan districts, but we know that the great urban concentration of the California population remains unaltered.

The urban character of the population of California becomes sharply revealed in all interstate comparisons. These are the chief differences:

a) The population of California, as compared with that of most other states, is characterized by smaller families. A rapidly decreasing sex ratio indicates increasing proportion of women to men in the total population.

b) There are fewer children in the population of California and a larger proportion of persons who are in the prime of life or are middle-aged.

c) A larger proportion of the adult population is at work in California, as compared with most of the other states, and a larger proportion of employed persons are white-collar workers.

d) The average income per capita is higher in California, but there is greater inequality in the distribution of incomes than in most of the other states.

These are urban characteristics shared by all populations in urban-industrial sections of the country. The early emergence of these characteristics in California and their present advanced development require no special theory of causation. They are consequences of the urbanization of the country as a whole. The particular manifestations of them in California find ready explanation in the migration differentials associated with urban development.

THE COURSE OF INTERNAL MIGRATION

California entered the continental economy of the United States during the opening years of an epoch characterized by the growing importance of cities (1840–1880). Throughout this entire period there was steady abandonment of farm lands in the older sections of the country, and a basic reorganization of economic life. In New York State alone, improved land was abandoned at the rate of 100,000 acres a year. The drift of the rural population into the cities and to the western lands gained momentum as the scope of this process widened.

Extensive application of machinery to agriculture, and the opening of virgin fields in Australia, the Argentine, and the American West rendered unnecessary and unprofitable much of the agricultural labor in Germany, France, and England. The profound social reorganization of Europe which resulted from these changes was in the background of migration to America. Such reorganization sometimes took place without immigration to the New World; but it was always attended by changes in population drift to the cities, a movement to waste lands or to other European countries. People went to the United States when American industry was prosperous, and each wave of migration coincided with an era of unusual business activity.

The European immigration to the United States and the shifting course of migration within the country itself were part of the same general movement, leading to the growth of cities and the industrialization of regions. In their cumulative effect they brought about wide differences in the distribution of resources and contributed to the establishment of wide differentials in regional economies.

In discussing international migration as it has affected the United States it is customary to reserve the term "immigration" to the movement of population during a period somewhat later than the American Revolution, characterized by individual as distinguished from group migration. In this later period, a distinction is made between the "old" migration from northern and western Europe and the "new" migration from southern and eastern Europe. This major shift in the pattern of European migration to the United States occurred during the last decade of the nineteenth century.

In the course of this migration, between the years 1815 and 1914, thirty-five million Europeans were added to the American population. This was as highly significant in determining the regional pattern of population distribution as the two centuries of colonization that preceded. This later phase of European migration was associated with the development of the North and the West.

The composition of the foreign-born population in the country as a whole has undergone a marked change since it was first enumerated in the census of 1850. At that time, 90 per cent of foreign-born were natives of northwestern Europe: the British Isles, Germany, the Scandinavian countries, the Low Countries, France, and Switzerland. Less than 1 per cent of the foreign-born enumerated in 1850 came from southern and eastern Europe. At the present time, the proportion from northwestern Europe has fallen to about 35 per cent and the proportion from southern and eastern Europe has increased to 40 per cent of the total of foreign-born. These changes in the pattern of international migration are reflected in California.

Table 8 shows the percentage of each foreign-born group in California in 1930 which migrated to the United States in 1900 or earlier. The foreign-born groups of longest residence in the United States are the Germans, the Scandinavians, and the Irish. More than half of the Germans, and nearly half of the Scandinavians, immigrated to the United States in 1900 or earlier. Mexicans are the most recent of any

TABLE 8

FOREIGN-BORN GROUPS IN CALIFORNIA, 1930: COUNTRY OF BIRTH
AND PERCENTAGE OF EACH THAT MIGRATED TO THE UNITED
STATES IN 1900 OR EARLIER

Country of birth	Percentage
Germany..................................	54.2
Scandinavian countries......................	47.6
Ireland...................................	44.6
France...................................	36.2
England, Wales, and Scotland................	33.1
Russia...................................	21.8
China....................................	20.8
Italy.....................................	18.4
Japan....................................	10.1
Mexico...................................	3.7

SOURCE: United States Census, 1930, Vol. II, pp. 512, 526.

of the immigrant groups. Of the persons born in Mexico now resident in California, less than 4 per cent arrived in the United States in 1900 or earlier; more than 40 per cent arrived in 1920 or later.

In the first census enumeration of California, in 1850, nearly one-fourth of the population was foreign-born. Persons born in Great Britain and Ireland, Germany, and France constituted nearly one-half of this foreign-born population. Between 1850 and 1860 the foreign-born population increased sharply, accounting for 39 per cent of the population of California. Thereafter the foreign-born population of California declined, constituting a steadily decreasing proportion of the total population. The proportion was 30 per cent in 1890, 22 per cent in 1920, and 13 per cent in 1940.

Throughout recent history the ebb and flow of immigration and the changing pattern of internal migration have moved in relation to each other. In reviewing the course of internal migration as it affected the settlement of California and the Pacific Coast it is necessary to keep in mind the connection between these two movements. The region of origin of European migration has shifted. In the different regions and countries of origin different segments of population were affected by

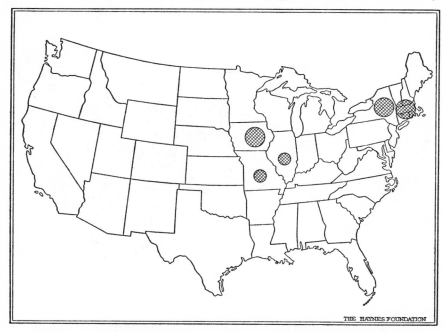

Fig. 4. Principal sources of migration to California, 1860–1870. Leading states: New York, Massachusetts, Iowa. Source: United States Census, 1860 and 1870.

this migration. There have been equally decisive shifts in the region of origin of migrants within the United States itself over the years. With each shift a different segment of the country's population was affected by the movement.

Recent experience on the Pacific Coast has led people to associate internal migration with destitution. Public comment on the problems of migrant population in recent years has inevitably associated internal migration with crisis situations of war and depression.

The series of maps in figures 4, 5, 6, and 8 illustrate some of the characteristics of this pattern for selected periods. For dates prior to the period 1935–1940, the identifications of the principal sources of migration are based on the state-of-birth data of successive censuses. This is a highly indirect method and is defective for the purpose at hand since the data do not include information on secondary movements between the state of birth and the state of residence at the time of the census. This, however, is a defect shared by later statistics on internal migration; and in the absence of direct statistics, state-of-

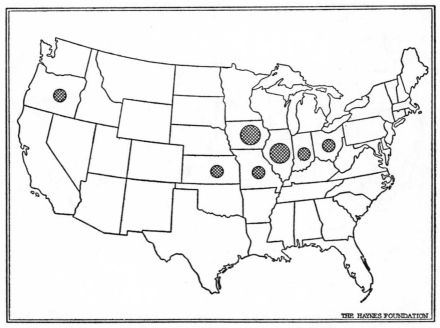

Fig. 5. Principal sources of migration to California, 1890–1900. Leading states: Illinois, Iowa. Source: United States Census, 1890 and 1900.

birth data provide important clues to the volume and direction of interstate movements of population.

On each map, the states indicated as principal sources of migration together account for approximately 50 per cent of the "net effective migration" from all the states to California. "Net effective migration," as defined by Weeks, is "the number of persons who have come into the state and have survived and remained to the end of the decade in excess of those of the California population who have moved away."[14]

_____

[14] David Weeks, *Permissible Economic Rate of Irrigation Development in California* (California Division of Water Resources, Bulletin No. 35, 1930), p. 36. A summary of census data on the residents of California by state, territory, and country of birth, showing net change between census years, appears in: Popu-

The westward migration of population during the 1930's, remarkable as it was, was by no means unprecedented in the history of the West. The largest migration to California, both in numbers and in relation to the population already in the state, took place between 1920 and 1930. During the ten-year period following 1920 there was a net addition by migration to the California population of more than two

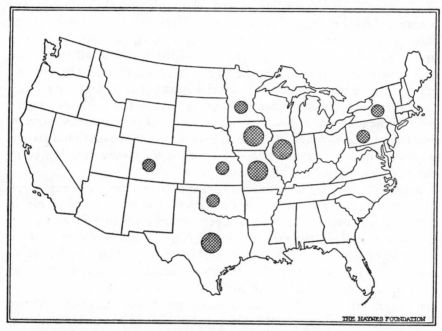

THE HAYNES FOUNDATION

Fig. 6. Principal sources of migration to California, 1920–1930. Leading states: Illinois, Missouri, Texas, Iowa. Source: United States Census, 1920 and 1930.

million, or a net gain of 60 per cent. During the 1930's, California received slightly less than one-half as many people as during the preceding decade. This represented a net addition of only 19 per cent to the total population.

The migration of the 1920's was part of the great drift of the population toward metropolitan centers. While metropolitan New York attracted one and one-half million persons, more than one and one-third million migrated into the Los Angeles area. The four areas of

lation Committee for the Central Valley Project Studies, *Statistical Memorandum No. 6*, by Charles N. Reynolds and Sara Miles (Berkeley, 1944), table 1, pp. 1–11. See also C. W. Thornthwaite, *Internal Migration in the United States* (Philadelphia, 1934), for an analysis of past migration based on the evidence of state-of-birth data for the country as a whole.

New York, Los Angeles, Chicago, and Detroit attracted four and one-half million persons—a figure more than half as great as the total number of persons who left the farms for the cities during the decade.[15]

In the United States at the present time, many more persons live in cities than on farms, and internal migration is far from being exclusively a movement from the farm to the city. Even the migration of the 1930's, so closely linked with the agricultural distress in the wheat and cotton areas of the southern plains, was not a movement of farm people alone. In this westward movement, persons engaged in agriculture constituted only a fraction of the total. Of all those who moved into California during the 1930's, only one-fifth had been farmers or farm laborers prior to migration. Actually, occupations other than farming were more heavily represented in the total movement than in the areas of origin. In all the states except Oklahoma, farmers and farm laborers tended to remain behind; other occupational groups tended to move in greater proportions than they were represented in the 1930 population of the various states.[16]

Migration into urban-industrial areas depends upon the expansion of employment opportunities in nonagricultural occupations. This, in turn, is a function of the business cycle and of economic development. Comparisons of the time pattern in the Negro migration with changes in the agricultural conditions and industrial labor demand, for example, lead to the conclusion that the agricultural factor apparently was not important in these movements. The industrial factor seems to be the dominant force in all the movements of the American Negro. There is reason to believe that, in general, both in-migration and out-migration increase with prosperity and decrease during depression. To an extreme degree, migration in depression years has been toward the worst land areas, to the very sections which past experience has shown to be least capable of providing a decent living. Cityward migration, therefore, is not a depression phenomenon. A high level of employment in California will be associated with continued in-migration. If there is to be any considerable return migration, this will take place with the decline of employment opportunities.

Studies of the 1940–1945 period now being made at the Bureau of the Census and elsewhere are beginning to reveal great similarities

[15] National Resources Committee, *The Problems of a Changing Population* (Washington, D.C., 1938), pp. 89–90.
[16] Seymour J. Janow, "Volume and Characteristics of Recent Migration to the Far West," in Committee on Interstate Migration of Destitute Citizens (Tolan Committee), *Hearings* (Washington, D.C., 1941), pp. 2299–2301.

between wartime migration and the patterns of population movement during the five years preceding it.[17] Migration patterns change relatively slowly because they are the outcome of persistent trends. What we are beginning to learn about wartime migration not only points to similarities with earlier periods, but strengthens the belief that the pattern of migration in the period immediately ahead will be the same.

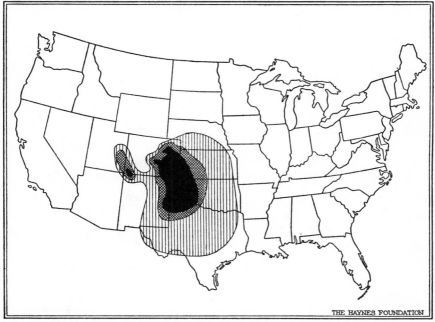

Fig. 7. Dust Bowl, 1932. Source: H. F. Choun, "Dust Storms in the Southwestern Plains Area," *Monthly Weather Review*, 64 (1936), p. 195.

The movement of population into California during the late thirties, then, is the pattern we should expect to prevail for some years to come.

A disastrous phase of the movement of the 1930's was the migration of destitute people from the southern plains. Although the greater proportion of this area had been in agricultural settlement for less than forty years, rapid mechanization of agriculture, and the consolidation of holdings that went with it, was introducing radical alterations in its economy. By 1930, the abandoning of land made worthless by erosion was turning huge stretches of the country, as in western Oklahoma,

---

[17] Henry S. Shryock, Jr., and Hope Tisdale Eldridge, "Internal Migration in Peace and War," *American Sociological Review*, 12 (1947), pp. 37–39.

into the wilderness of the Dust Bowl. Oklahoma, with a great circle of territory surrounding it, became the focal point of one of the most spectacular population movements in the country's history.

California received the greater part of this population, but the Dust Bowl migration was only an episode in the total movement that took place during the 1930's. It is true that the 95,000 migrants from

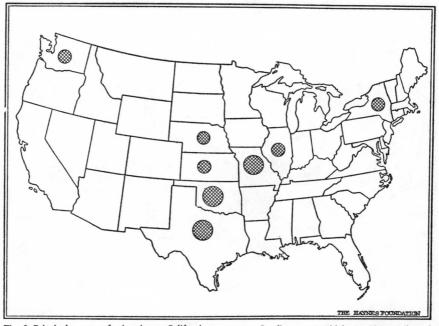

Fig. 8. Principal sources of migration to California, 1935–1940. Leading states: Oklahoma, Texas, Missouri. Source: United States Census, 1940.

Oklahoma to California exceeded the number moving between any other two states; and Texas was next, sending 68,000. But Missouri, Illinois, and New York ranked next after Oklahoma and Texas in the number of migrants to California; each of twenty-six other states contributed 10,000 or more to the total movement.[18]

This was, in the main, an urban migration. Seventy per cent of the migrants moved into the cities and small towns of the state; the city of Los Angeles alone received one-third of this urban movement. Most of the migrants who moved into the rural areas were from predominantly rural sections of the country—Oklahoma, Texas, Missouri,

[18] *Ibid.*, pp. 29-30.

TABLE 9
LEADING STATES OF MIGRATION TO CALIFORNIA, 1935–1940

California			Rural territory		
State	Number	Per cent	State	Number	Per cent
All states.......	876,829	100.0	All states......	280,624	100.0
Oklahoma......	94,668	10.8	Oklahoma.....	57,235	20.4
Texas..........	67,936	7.8	Texas.........	27,827	9.9
Missouri.......	57,953	6.6	Missouri......	19,180	6.8
Illinois.........	51,850	5.9	Arkansas......	18,285	6.5
New York......	46,137	5.3	Kansas........	14,388	5.1
Kansas.........	42,386	4.8	Arizona.......	12,633	4.5
Nebraska.......	39,121	4.5	Oregon........	12,037	4.3
Washington.....	38,769	4.4	Colorado......	10,374	3.7
Colorado......	34,263	3.9	Nebraska......	9,821	3.5
Oregon.........	32,336	3.7	Washington....	9,120	3.3

Los Angeles			San Francisco		
State	Number	Per cent	State	Number	Per cent
All states.......	224,049	100.0	All states......	42,567	100.0
New York......	21,452	9.6	Washington....	5,421	12.7
Illinois.........	21,212	9.5	New York.....	3,885	9.1
Texas..........	16,729	7.5	Oregon........	3,547	8.3
Missouri.......	15,962	7.1	Illinois........	3,082	7.3
Oklahoma......	12,395	5.5	Missouri......	1,856	4.4
Nebraska.......	10,651	4.7	Texas.........	1,796	4.2
Kansas.........	9,895	4.4	Utah..........	1,690	4.0
Iowa..........	8,758	3.9	Colorado......	1,554	3.7
Ohio..........	8,687	3.9	Nebraska......	1,543	3.6
Colorado.......	8,549	3.8	Minnesota.....	1,402	3.3

SOURCE: United States Census, 1940.

Arkansas, Kansas were prominent among states of origin. Movement to Los Angeles was predominantly an urban movement. The largest group of migrants to Los Angeles came from New York and Illinois. San Francisco attracted migrants from Washington and Oregon as well as from Illinois and New York.

In table 9, the leading states of migration to Los Angeles, San Francisco, and the rural territories are listed and compared with the statistics for the state as a whole.

These migration statistics for cities are not altogether satisfactory, since the available census data are for the central cities alone, whereas the entire urban agglomeration surrounding the central city should be the basis of comparison. But differences of the sources of migration for the cities and rural territory indicate that the population movement of the 1930's was made up of streams of migration involving different population groups and different social areas of the country. The circumstances surrounding the movement of each of these groups were different from one another. They entered the California society at different levels and they now occupy in it vastly different positions.

In the earlier periods, other sections and other states had been the significant focal points of migration. The Middle West, and, in that section, Illinois and Iowa, may be taken as representative of the areas of out-migration for the important population movement that took place in the twenties. In the migration of the sixties and seventies, New York and the New England States were among the leading states.

The circumstances surrounding the population movement have differed markedly in each one of these episodes in the migration history of California. Movement out of New England and New York State was a consequence of a profound economic reorganization in the country. An entire period until about 1840 had been characterized by almost complete decentralization of social life in the East. In New York State alone there were 900 miles of canals, 6,000 waterwheels, 400 small industrial centers in small towns scattered through the farming area. The economic reorganization that took place during the forties and fifties ended with the disappearance of this town-centered life. Before 1850, the Erie Canal served the local communities in New York State. After 1850, it became important for interstate traffic. The abandonment of vast areas of farm land during that period was associated with these developments.[19]

The movement out of the Middle West was associated with the long period of rising land values in the corn belt. In a recent study of the contemporary culture of Irwin, Iowa, one student had occasion to describe the events of that period:

Beef cattle prices between 1897 and 1920 skyrocketed from 6 cents to 10, 12, 15, 18, 20 cents and even more, per pound. Hog prices rose from 4 cents

---

[19] These phases in the development of the State of New York have been outlined by Henry Wright in New York State Commission of Housing and Regional Planning, *Final Report* (Albany, 1926).

to 7, 10, 13, 15, 17, 18 cents. Prices for corn rose from 25 cents a bushel to 45, 75, 90, $1, and finally $2 a bushel. The price of land followed the commodity market up, from $20 an acre to $35, $50, $100, $200, $400, $500.

Census figures of average farm value, including land and building, show clearly what had taken place. In 1860, the average value per farm was $1,418. This·had increased to $2,447 by 1870, and to $2,460 by 1880. In 1890, the figures stood at $4,125. By 1900, it had reached $6,800.

The average value per farm in 1910 skyrocketed to $21,362 and this was only the beginning. The figure reached $54,125 in 1920. Farmers having lived through the experience could not believe that things could be otherwise. They argued that certain years might bring lower prices but the passing decades always found prices of farm land going higher.

The crash came with alarming suddenness. The prices of cattle, hogs, corn and land all tumbled together in 1920's.[20]

The Middle West's out-migration reached a peak at the end of this long speculative period in farming.

Each of these episodes of migration brought to California people with a different background of social experience and organization. The groups differed from one another in population history, in their framework of attitudes, motivations, and purposes. Each of these episodes of migration was a movement to the cities and small towns of the state. Each represented a distinct stream contributing to the making of the urban character of California.

The migration history of the state and of its distinctive sections, north and south, is undoubtedly far more complex than this. But our drastic condensation and oversimplification of what is admittedly a vastly more complex process is deliberate. The three episodes of California migration have thus been presented in their essential elements to suggest what the meaning of the shifting course of migration during the hundred-year history of California might be. Each episode made a significant contribution to the structuring of California population, each wave of migration had a markedly different influence on the population make-up of California, each group has played, and is now playing, a markedly different role in its population history. The relation of all of this to social differentiation and to stratification in California cities is obvious, but we do not know a great deal about it. The detailed analysis of this relationship is among the critical needs in the study of our cities.

[20] Edward O. Moe and Carl C. Taylor, *Culture of a Contemporary Rural Community: Irwin, Iowa* (Washington, D.C., 1942), pp. 9–10.

Part One

VARIATIONS IN THE SOCIAL CHARACTERISTICS OF THE POPULATION OF LOS ANGELES

II. The Variables and Their Measurement

THIS STUDY is chiefly concerned with the description and measurement of social differentiation associated with the urban phenomenon of Los Angeles. Mass statistics of the urban area are used to establish group characteristics and to reveal the broad regularities of social differentiation for the population as a whole. So far as the statistics used have a geographic frame of reference, the differences in the social characteristics of the population are located by reference to geography. The primary interest, however, is not in the spatial distribution of social phenomena, but in the structure of the urban society itself, and no assumptions are made about spatial relations as determinants of the differences that are being examined. Later, when social areas are identified, it will be because of convenience in conceiving of social organization as involving structure and position and social relations as taking place within a given social space.

The basis of this study is an analysis of population and housing data by census tracts for the entire Los Angeles area falling within Los Angeles County. The variables chosen for examination are derived from the tract data of the 16th Census of the United States, 1940. The use of the 1940 census as a source is justified because it is the most recent complete census of population we have, and the objective is to reveal the broad regularities governing the variations in the social characteristics of the population.

If each census tract in an urban area is viewed as a discrete unit and the population characteristics are examined in detail in isolation from those of other groups, the diversity and range of variation encountered become astonishing and disconcerting. If we do this in Los Angeles and examine the 570-odd census tracts of the area as things in themselves, we may easily be tempted to agree with the statement, which is often made, that Los Angeles is "different" or "unique" and that no coherent urban form or structure is to be discovered in its development.

Statistics referring to the social characteristics of a single urban tract or a given population group, although significant as information, are devoid of any larger meaning unless they can be viewed in their relation to the characteristics of other census tracts or other population groups within the same urban system.

By the very nature of the material to be examined this presupposes a statistical study. The essential characteristic of a statistical study is not that it employs numerical computation, but that it deals with groups and with mass phenomena. Conclusions of a statistical study apply to a group as a whole, and not necessarily to some selected member of that group.

When the social characteristics of urban populations are studied statistically, it is observed that they follow certain broad regularities, and that the variations in social characteristics are graded and measurable. When different attributes of a population are isolated or measured, they are found to vary in relation to other attributes of the same population in some orderly manner. Moreover, it is found that the broad regularities in the distribution of social characteristics of urban populations are regularities of the same general type as are encountered in the statistical studies of larger population groupings in the country as a whole.

In dealing with the simultaneous variation of mutually dependent variables, it is methodologically desirable to think of these variables as constituting a system. A system so conceived is plainly a fiction, a conceptual scheme designed to serve as a framework of analysis and description. In such a system certain of the variables will have greater analytic significance than others, and a description of the general relation of these primary variables will also be a summary of the conditions in the system. In such a description the enumeration of factors will necessarily be incomplete, but it is ordinarily necessary to consider at least certain of the key factors, and sometimes no more need be considered.[1]

The variables we have chosen for emphasis in this study are seven, three related in a composite index of social rank, three related in a composite index of urbanization, and one used as a simple index of segregation.

The three variables related in the index of social rank refer to occupational status, educational status, and income. Occupational status is measured by the number of craftsmen, operatives, and laborers,

---

[1] For a detailed discussion of the concepts involved, see L. J. Henderson, *Pareto's General Sociology— A Physiologist's Interpretation* (Harvard University Press, 1935).

related to the number of employed persons. Educational status is measured by the number of persons who had completed grade school or less in relation to the number of persons twenty-five years old and over. Income is indicated by rent per capita, the total monthly contract or estimated rent related to the total population.

In order to weight equally each of these factors in a composite index, the values for each variable were converted to percentile scores relative to the range of each. Zero indicates lowest status value, and 100 highest. The mean percentile score for the three variables is the index of social rank for each census tract. A low index indicates many craftsmen, operatives, and laborers, many persons who had completed grade school only, and low rent. A high index indicates few craftsmen, operatives, and laborers, few persons who had completed grade school only, and high rent.

The three variables related in the index of urbanization refer to fertility, women in the labor force, and the physical character of neighborhoods. Fertility is measured by the number of children under five years in relation to women of childbearing ages (15–44). The number of women in the labor force is related to women fourteen years old and over. The percentage of dwelling units which are single-family detached is taken as an indication of the physical character of neighborhoods.

Values for each of these variables were converted to percentiles of their ranges. The mean of the three percentile scores is the index of urbanization for each census tract. A low index indicates high fertility, few women in the labor force, and many single-family detached dwelling units. A high index shows low fertility, many women in the labor force, and few single-family dwelling units.

The variable used as an index of segregation is the number of persons in highly isolated population groups in relation to the total population. Groups have been considered highly isolated if their average proportions in the populations of neighborhoods where they live are equal to three or more times their respective proportions in the population of the county. The population groups include Negroes, Mexicans and Mexican-Americans, Orientals, and persons born in Russia and Italy.

The use of these three indexes—social rank, urbanization, and segregation—in the development of a typology is discussed in chapter vi, "Elements of an Urban Typology."

Map presentation of data.—For the purpose of map presentation of the census-tract data, a base map was developed which included only the residential occupied area of the tracts. Heretofore, no map of this description was available for the Los Angeles area. Consequently, when social data were shown by census tracts in map form with color or hachure, vacant land, sparsely settled land, and land used for industrial and recreational purposes were indicated as possessing social characteristics typical of residential areas. This distortion is avoided by using a residential occupied area base map.

In maps shown in figure 9 (facing this page), figure 10 (facing p. 38), figure 12 (facing p. 42), figure 23 (facing p. 70), and figure 64 (facing p. 160) this base is used. In figure 64, census-tract boundaries which coincide with boundaries of 185 named places are shown in addition to the residential occupied area. The generalized highway map used as base in figure 11 (facing p. 40) is adapted from a similarly generalized map of the Automobile Club of Southern California.

In figure 18 (facing p. 56) the base is a composite of a series of maps of the Los Angeles County Regional Planning Commission which show railroads and major industrial areas, including oil fields. Figure 63 (facing p. 148) is adapted from the census-tract map in the same series.

The scale of all maps is approximately five miles to the inch. It should be emphasized, however, that this graphic material, though in map form, is essentially diagrammatic; the maps are not intended to be used in the precise location of items shown.

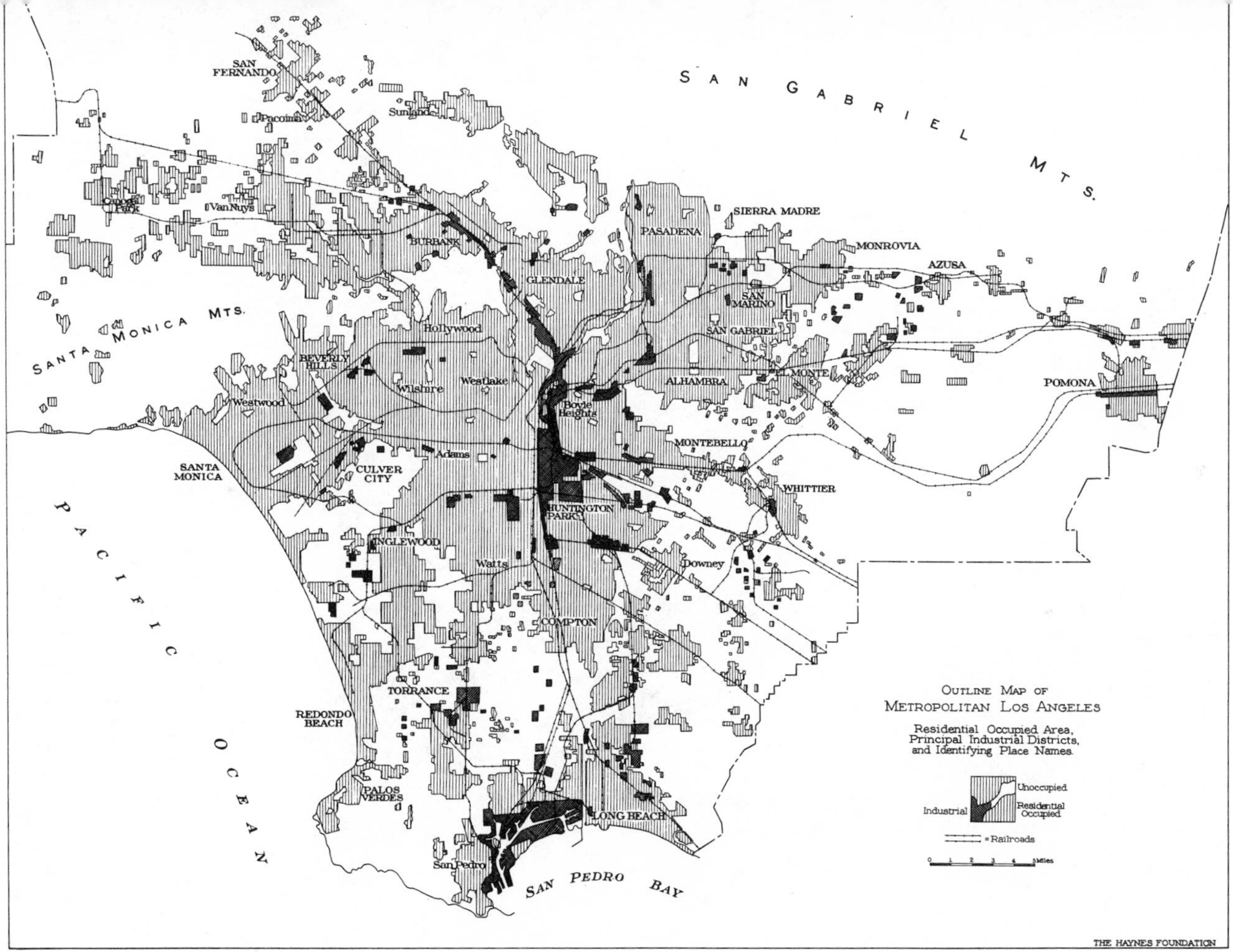

OUTLINE MAP OF
METROPOLITAN LOS ANGELES

Residential Occupied Area,
Principal Industrial Districts,
and Identifying Place Names

Industrial
Residential
Occupied
Unoccupied

⸻⸻ Railroads

0   1   2   3   4   5 Miles

Fig. 9. Outline map of Metropolitan Los Angeles.

III. Social Rank

B<small>Y</small> "<small>SOCIAL RANK</small>" we mean the differential standing of persons or groups in a system of social positions. Every society, whether made up of small numbers and simple in its organization, or the result of the coming together of very large numbers with a complex organization, evolves social patterns to guide the reciprocal behavior of its members. The functioning of every human organization, of every society, depends on the presence of these patterns for living together.[1] Rank is the place occupied by individuals or groups of individuals within this pattern.

Following Kingsley Davis,[2] we use "position" as the broadest and most inclusive concept here. Since by "position" is meant a place in a given social structure, it is well to remember that social structure is not a concrete reality, but emerges from the observable behavior of the members of society.

The variables we have chosen as indicators of position in society are important factors in social stratification. Neither the data at our disposal nor the procedures we have used, however, permit us to go far in an analysis of stratification in urban society. The term "social rank" is, therefore, used in a strictly limited sense, without the connotation of social class.[3]

HIERARCHY OF OCCUPATIONS

Occupation, income, and education may be taken as chief indicators of position in society. This is because modern society is organized on an occupational basis, and income is roughly correlated with occupation. Education, or level of schooling, as an element of social distinction is a function of the increasing occupational organization of society and the growing stress on professional training and skill in all walks of life.

It is a matter of common observation that occupations are evaluated and generally accorded honor and esteem on a scale of prestige which corresponds to their relative importance as determinants of social position. This is recognized by everyone, and influences behavior.

[1] See Ralph Linton, *The Study of Man* (New York, 1936), pp. 98–106.
[2] "A Conceptual Analysis of Stratification," *American Sociological Review*, 7 (1942), pp. 309–310.
[3] The term "social class" is frequently applied to the status system of modern urban society. In this sense the term would appear to have limited application. The status system of modern society is a social continuum; there are no natural class boundaries susceptible of objective definition.

Relations among occupations in a complex society may best be understood if occupations are conceived as positions within a system. Occupational structure, so conceived, implies a hierarchy of functions. In the Yankee City studies, Warner and Srole presented such a conceptual framework for the understanding of the occupational evaluation of groups in the modern American community.[4] For this purpose, they arranged occupations appearing in the small New England town they studied into "three broad, widely recognized hierarchical categories according to types of techniques." The elements of their scheme may be given in highly condensed form, with the categories of occupations arranged in ascending order, as follows:

I. Manual techniques:
    A. Unskilled labor
    B. Skilled factory operations
    C. Skilled craft operations
II. Exchange-control techniques—"white collar" occupations:
    A. Management-aid operations, supervisors, foremen, salesmen
    B. Management operations, administration. Control of the market and factory
III. Professional techniques—involving advanced knowledge directed toward highly important group functions:
    Law, medicine, technical and symbolic creations: engineers, scientists, artists

Approaching the problem of the hierarchy of occupations for the purpose of another type of research, Raymond Pearl developed a classification and code of occupations in which he grouped all occupations under three general headings:

I. Owners, managers, officials, and professional men
II. Skilled and semiskilled professional workers
III. Laborers—unskilled and semiskilled[5]

The underlying idea of Pearl's classification was "to contrast *primarily* two groups of persons, namely those (I) who, on the whole, are situated at or near the top of things in the existing social organization, and those (III) who by and large find themselves at or near the bottom in the same social organization. This leaves a third class (II), persons who are, on the whole, neither very near the top or the

[4] W. Lloyd Warner and Leo Srole, *The Social Systems of American Ethnic Groups* (New Haven, 1945), pp. 56–58.
[5] Raymond Pearl, "A Classification and Code of Occupations," *Human Biology*, 5 (1933), p. 493.

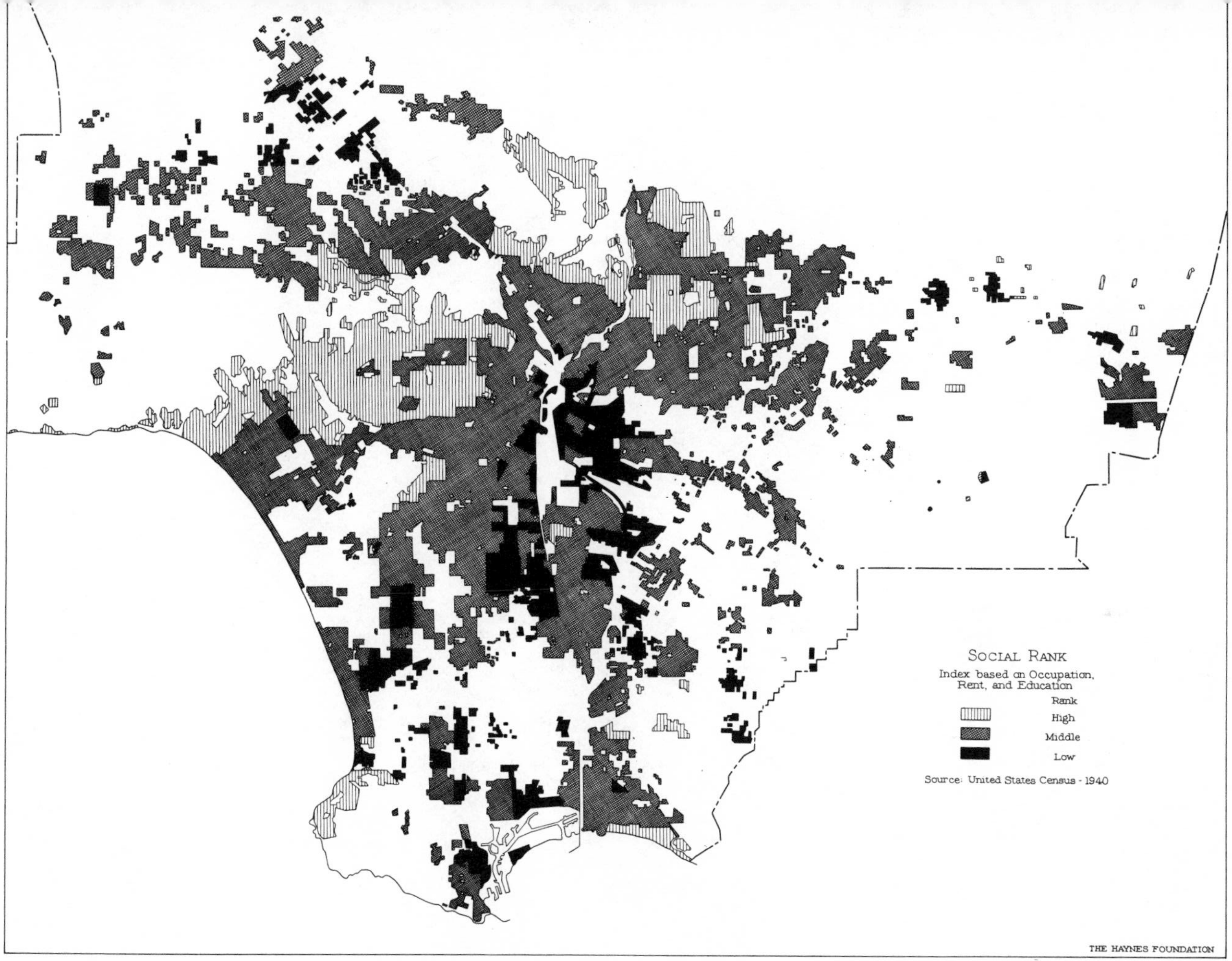
SOCIAL RANK
Index based on Occupation, Rent, and Education
Rank
High
Middle
Low
Source: United States Census - 1940
THE HAYNES FOUNDATION

Fig. 10. Map showing three levels of social rank.

bottom, and who, as they are sometimes thought and sometimes think themselves to be worse off than those in Class I, are plainly and admittedly better off, on the whole, than those in Class III."

Pearl pointed to the distinction between I and III as a real and fundamental one, but stressed that the distinction was to be made in a statistical sense. "The individuals falling statistically into any particular occupational subrubric—say, for example, 'undertakers'—are not all precisely alike in circumstances and attitude. The whole enterprise of the classification and the subsequent tabulation of occupational data is bound to be a *statistical* one, as distinct from an individualistic one with unvarying precision of mathematical relationships."[6]

Census officials were among the first persons in the United States to recognize the importance of classifying occupations into socially meaningful categories. It was not until the late 1930's, however, that a social-economic grouping of occupations was made available by the Bureau of the Census. In the current organizations of the census material the work of Alba M. Edwards[7] has had the most far-reaching influence.

The United States Census classifies employed persons by industries and by types of occupation. By reclassifying census categories, Alba Edwards and others have developed groupings of gainful workers according to social-economic gradations. The following listing of occupations drawn from the population statistics of the census represents a regrouping of urban workers in descending order of social rank:

Professionals and proprietors:
  Professional workers
  Semiprofessional workers
  Proprietors, managers, and officials

Clerical and domestic workers:
  Clerical, sales, and kindred workers
  Domestic-service workers
  Service workers, except domestic

Craftsmen, operatives, and laborers:
  Craftsmen, foremen, and kindred workers
  Operatives and kindred workers
  Laborers

[6] *Ibid.*, pp. 493–495.
[7] *A Social-Economic Grouping of the Gainful Workers of the United States, 1930*, Bureau of the Census (Washington, D.C., 1938).

Craftsmen, operatives, and laborers, although not altogether a homogeneous group, stand in the lowest relative position in the hierarchy of occupations, and their distribution may be taken as an indicator of the occupational level of the population in each tract.

To measure the variations in the social position of populations over the range encountered in the urban area, a composite index is used. The variables combined in this index—the number of craftsmen, operatives, and laborers, the number of persons with grade-school education only, and rent per capita as a measure of income—are related to social rank in the following manner:

The number of craftsmen, operatives, and laborers (occupation ratio) is inversely related to social rank. The smaller the number, the higher the social rank of the population.

The number of persons in a population completing grade school only (education ratio) is inversely related to social rank. The smaller the number of persons completing grade school only, the higher the social position.

Rent per capita as a measure of income is directly related to social rank. The higher the rent per capita for a given population, the higher the social rank.

The percentile score for the occupation ratio is combined with the percentile scores for the education ratio and for rent per capita in the index of social rank for each census tract. The distribution of census tracts at three levels of social rank is shown in figure 10.

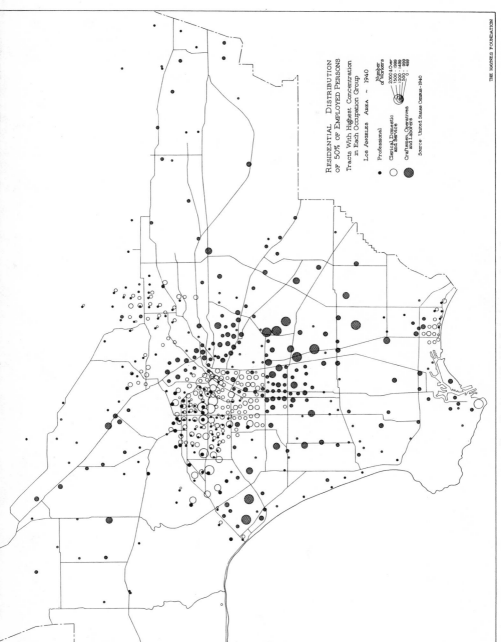

RESIDENTIAL DISTRIBUTION
OF 50% OF EMPLOYED PERSONS

Tracts With Highest Concentration
in Each Occupation Group

LOS ANGELES AREA – 1940

Number
of Workers

2000 & Over
1500 - 1999
1000 - 1499
500 - 999
0 - 499

Professional

Clerical, Domestic
and Service

Craftsmen, Operatives
and Laborers

Source United States Census -1940

Fig. 11. Map showing residential distribution of 50 per cent of employed persons.

IV. Urbanization

In the chapter dealing with social rank we considered the relative position of occupations on a scale of rank and prestige. We there used the distribution of one category of occupied persons as the key term in an index of social position. We did not consider the other social characteristics of any of the occupation groups.

In figure 11, based on the same occupation statistics, a similar range of data is presented for another purpose. Here the residential distribution of the three occupation groups is shown in terms of areas of their greatest concentration. The relative social position of these two segments of the urban area is not the point to be made from what this map presents, although that relationship is one inference to be drawn from it. The point to be made is the fact that the employed persons thus shown to be residentially differentiated exhibit great differences of another sort. These differences are sharply revealed in the age and sex compositions of the populations involved. The working population in one segment is largely masculine and heavily weighted in favor of children and younger-age groups. The working population in the other segment, if not preponderantly feminine, is heavily weighted with younger women in paid employment, a larger proportion of persons in working ages, and fewer children.

Of the two major segments shown on the diagram, one is an area of high fertility associated with lower-level occupations, the other an area of low fertility associated with white-collar occupations and professional and managerial skills. The area of low fertility is the typical urban area of our society. The group characteristics of the population in this area derive from the steady drift of young women to the cities and the spread of the small-family system. These two elements in the character of this area are intimately associated with the present urban pattern of the distributive and service functions. This is typically the apartment-house district of the city. It is here that the changing character of the urban household finds its reflection in the elaborate development of urban services.

This is the great area of consumption in the city. It is preëminently the area of the chain store, the department store, and the open-air market. It is one major area of the city where life and work literally center around the market. It is the chief outlet for the mass-produced consumers' goods. The mass media of advertising and communication direct their appeal here. This is where, in large measure, the great leveling of urban standards and tastes takes place, where urban attitudes of emulation, conspicuous display, and wastefulness are best observed.

When we single out the ratio of children to women as a differential in urbanization, we do so on the basis of the recognition that fertility is not an isolated variable. It is one of a complex of interdependent variables. Its variations are intimately linked with variations in the age structure of the population and the changing pattern of the family, and is largely controlled by the prevailing standards, attitudes, and needs.

Within the conceptual framework of our analysis it is not permissible to consider populations of low and high fertility marked out in this generalization as polar types. The polar opposite of a highly urban population is a population highly rural in character, not to be found in California at all. The two populations contrasted in their fertility in our generalization represent variations within a single urban pattern.

To measure the degree of urbanization of different population groups over the range of variation encountered in the urban area, a composite index is used. The variables combined in this index—fertility, women in the labor force, and single-family dwelling units—are related to urbanization in the following manner:

The ratio of children to women, or fertility, is inversely related to urbanization; the lower the fertility, the higher the degree of urbanization.

The population of women in paid occupations (women in the labor force) is directly related to urbanization. The higher the proportion of women in paid occupations, in the total population of women fourteen years old or over, the higher the urbanization.

The proportion of dwellings which are single-family units is inversely related to urbanization. The lower the proportion of single-family dwelling units, the higher the urbanization.

The relation of single-family dwelling units to urbanization may be viewed in a number of ways. It is customary to think of it in connection with home ownership and possible stability of residence. Some may consider its effect on the density of population. Neither of these considerations determined our choice of this measure. As we intend to use it, the declining proportion of the single-family dwelling unit is a

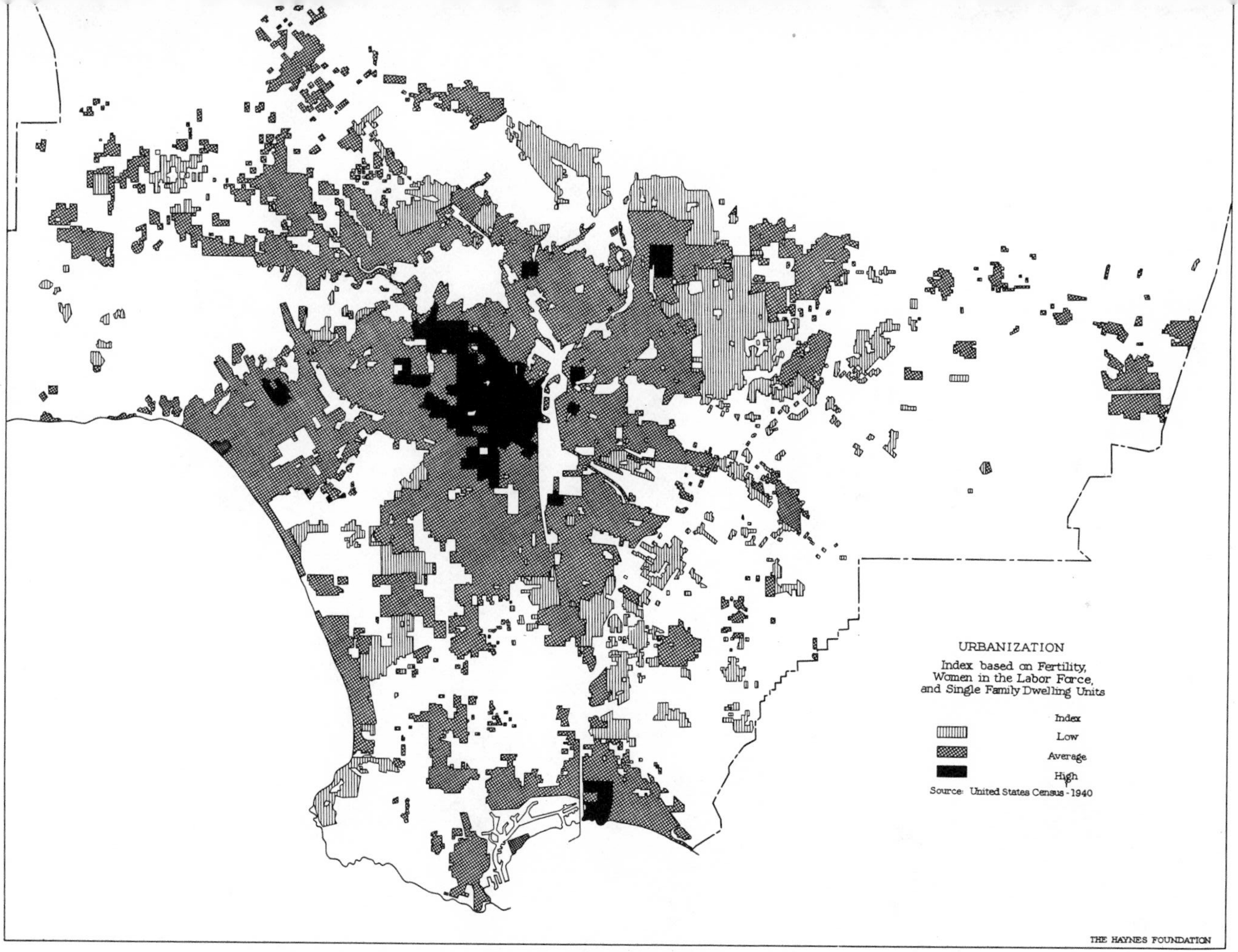
URBANIZATION
Index based on Fertility, Women in the Labor Force, and Single Family Dwelling Units
Index
Low
Average
High
Source: United States Census - 1940
THE HAYNES FOUNDATION

Fig. 12. Map showing three levels of urbanization.

rough measure of changes taking place in the functions of the household. Where the single-family unit is least numerous there is likely to be the greatest dependence on outside services for many of the household functions.

DIFFERENCES IN FERTILITY

Since 1910 there has been only one year during which deaths exceeded births in Los Angeles County—1918, at the time of an influenza epidemic. In every year since 1910, with the exception of that single year, births exceeded deaths by an appreciable margin. The margin of births over deaths rose to a peak around 1925, and then steadily declined, reaching a low point in 1935. Since then, it has been on the increase and is now steadily rising. In the recent report of the Survey of Hospital Facilities in Los Angeles,[1] vital statistics have been assembled by broad areas in the entire southern half of the county. The birth rates reported are uniformly higher than the death rates in every one of the areas considered. Yet there is hardly a population of any size in the county in which the number of children born per mother is sufficient to replace the present population.

Los Angeles, like most other large urban centers, has more births than deaths because of the concentration of young adults in cities. In 1940, persons between the ages of twenty and forty-four constituted nearly 40 per cent of total population in Los Angeles. This is typical of all cities, and it is this high proportion of young adults that serves to maintain a relatively high birth rate and a relatively low death rate in cities at the present time.

Under these conditions a population may, for the moment, sustain or even increase the number of its members by a balance of annual births over annual deaths while it may be failing to reproduce itself. In 1940 the proportion of married women aged 40–44 who were childless was 18.0 per cent in New York City, 19.0 per cent in Chicago, 28.5 per cent in Los Angeles. When a proportionate number of married women 40–44 not reporting on numbers of children born and the unmarried women of the same ages are added to this childless group, 29 per cent of the white women 40–44 in New York and Chicago, and 36 per cent of those in Los Angeles never had children.[2]

Within the Los Angeles urban area, as in all other metropolitan

---

[1] Los Angeles County-wide Hospital Survey, *A Hospital Plan for Los Angeles County,* by James A. Hamilton and Associates (Los Angeles, 1947).
[2] *16th Census of the United States, 1940,* "Population, Differential Fertility, 1940 and 1910: Fertility for States and Larger Cities," table 40, pp. 221–222.

areas, there may be found the widest possible differences in fertility as measured by the proportion of children to women. Table 10 gives examples.

In an earlier section dealing with the declining proportion of children, it was pointed out that the proportion of children to women, which is a true measure of the fertility of populations, exhibited wide

TABLE 10

PROPORTION OF CHILDREN TO WOMEN IN SELECTED PLACES IN
LOS ANGELES, 1940

Place	Number of children under 5 per 1,000 women 15–44
Hollywood...............................	67
Bunker Hill..............................	71
Beverly-Fairfax..........................	91
Beverly Hills............................	93
Huntington Park.........................	166
Whittier................................	173
Boyle Heights...........................	238
Maywood-Bell...........................	294
San Gabriel.............................	359
Gardena................................	380
Belvedere...............................	484
Watts (census tract 287).................	546

SOURCE: United States Census, 1940.

rural-urban differentials, and varied with occupation and income. The wide fertility differences observed in the Los Angeles area are directly related to the existing differences in income and occupational levels and provide a clue to the social position and the degree of urbanization of population groups concerned.[3]

Fertility is highest among populations at the lowest occupation and income levels, and at lowest level of schooling. It steadily declines with rising occupational level and increasing income, and reaches its lowest point among white-collar workers and professional groups.

[3] For differentials in other census-tract cities, see P. K. Whelpton, "Geographic and Economic Differentials in Fertility," *Annals of the American Academy of Political and Social Science*, 188 (November, 1936), pp. 48–51.

Women in Paid Employment

If women work less at home, it is because home has ceased to be a workplace. To a greater degree, this is true also of men.

The need for women's work in the present-day industrial structure is measured by the labor-force participation of women. Certain basic developments in the economy are in the background of increased participation of women in the labor force:

1. Gradual transition from home to factory production. This is still taking place.
2. Transition from home to factory production has meant the decline of the home as an economic unit where formerly many goods and services for the family's use were produced by women members.
3. Large-scale enterprise concerned with cost, production, and sales controls, marketing, administration, and a host of jobs clustering about the productive processes requires an elaborate structure of paper work. In this work women's labor is used.
4. Changes in social habits have led to the growth of new industries: laundries, beauty shops, restaurants, department stores. Labor-force participation of women has been greatest in these areas of employment.

Women are found in practically every one of the 450-odd occupational classifications used in 1940, but they are for the most part concentrated in only 23 occupations.[4] One-third or more of all employed persons in the following occupations in the United States are women:

Occupation	Percentage of women employed in 1940
Stenographers, typists, and secretaries	93.5
Servants	91.3
Operatives, apparel and accessories	77.5
Teachers	75.7
Bookkeepers, accountants, and cashiers	52.1
Clerical workers	35.7

The concentration of women in specific industries in California and Los Angeles is shown in table 11.

The pattern of women's participation in the labor force is given, in large part, by the pressures and opportunities of urban life. Three-

[4] Frieda S. Miller, "Women in the Labor Force," *Annals of the American Academy of Political and Social Science*, 251 (May, 1947), pp. 35–43.

fourths of all women who work for pay live in towns and cities, and fully one-half of these are single women. The largest participation by women in the labor force is in the great metropolitan centers. The proportion of women in the labor force decreases as the size of the city decreases. Least participation by women in the labor force is in rural areas.

Although there has been a very great increase in the participation by married women in the labor force, a relatively small proportion of

TABLE 11

RATIO OF WOMEN TO ALL PRODUCTION WORKERS, MAY, 1947

Industry	California	Los Angeles
	per cent	*per cent*
Apparel......................	80.8	80.3
Tobacco......................	71.2	84.5
Laundries.....................	69.7	69.4
Textile.......................	50.4	64.5
Insurance.....................	56.0	56.0
Leather.......................	41.0	51.7
Cleaning and dyeing	54.6	51.6
Paper........................	30.9	30.4

SOURCE: California Department of Industrial Relations, Division of Labor Statistics and Research, *Employment of Women in California*, May, 1947.

married women work. In 1940 only 15 per cent of all married women were at work in paid jobs. Compared with this, 46 per cent of all single women, and 30 per cent of the widowed and divorced, were working for pay. Here also, urbanization makes for greater participation in the labor force. Single urban women eighteen to forty-five years of age were not far behind men in the same age categories in their market participation in 1940.

On the average, mothers with young children are less likely to work than others. The long-term tendency in the country as a whole, however, is in the direction of increasing participation of married women in the labor force.[5]

[5] Hazel Kirk, "Who Works and Why," *Annals of the American Academy of Political and Social Science*, 251 (May, 1947), pp. 44-52.

V. Segregation

HERE WE ARE concerned with isolation as a group phenomenon susceptible of objective definition. As a group phenomenon, isolation of like forms occurs everywhere in nature. Its mechanisms and its mode of operation as a factor in evolution have been studied thoroughly. The possible bearing of the findings of population geneticists to problems of isolation in human society is a field in which there is considerable scope for play of opinion and prejudice. Isolation as a group phenomenon in human society is undoubtedly the result of a far more complex set of circumstances than the types of isolation observed in plant and animal communities.

In a society resulting from the coming together of individuals of diverse origins, backgrounds, and of differing interests, there is isolation of individuals of similar origin and position. Urban society is a heterogeneous society of this sort. It is the result of change and movement. In urban society, isolation of groups is a direct consequence of migration.

In a rapidly expanding urban environment the isolation of groups creates acute social needs tending toward the creation of instruments of cohesion and solidarity. Carey McWilliams has recently shown[1] that out of such acute needs in an earlier phase of population movement the "state society" emerged as a unique social institution of southern California and, for a time, even became a factor in the political life of the state. Beneath the ebb and flow of these institutional forms, however, the sense of isolation of the newcomer in a strange town continues. Almost on any week end, one can turn to the newspapers of Los Angeles and note in the calendar of events announcements of meetings of residents from particular towns in Indiana, Oregon, Ohio, or some other part of the country.

The urban dweller, as ideally conceived, is an individual who no longer identifies himself with kin or neighbor; his associations are determined by the variety of his own special interests and needs. He joins one group for economic reasons, another for purposes of recreation, still another on the basis of some further special interest. This

---

[1] *Southern California Country* (New York, 1946), pp. 165–175.

urban stereotype which finds support in economic dogma as well as in sociological doctrine causes us to underrate the part played by primary group ties in determining the individual's course of action in achieving rational ends.

Movement of factory workers and the migration of people in search of economic opportunity are actions to achieve such rational ends. Newer knowledge gained through studies in specific local areas suggests that family ties and ties of friendship are highly determinant in the direction of these movements.

In a study of a New England industrial community, Myers and MacLaurin found that the movement of factory workers tended to occur in neighborhood clusters. As they report their findings: "Firms in the plastic industry were located in one part of the community, and in the immediate neighborhood were companies manufacturing apparel, converted paper products, and furniture. More than 70 per cent of the moves recorded in the sample during 1937–1939 occurred between firms in these four industries. In another part of the community, the three shoe and leather products companies were situated in a large building which was a few blocks from cotton yarn mills and next door to the largest metal products firm. As in the plastics group, the number of workers who moved among these companies was much greater than the number who left their jobs for more distant parts of the community."[2]

A survey of migration and resettlement during the 1930's, reported on by Goldschmidt, inquired into the motives that prompted the migrants to come to California and to live in the towns in which they settled.[3] Out of forty-five families in one sample, thirty-five of those who came to California seeking work opportunities learned of these from relatives and friends, and fourteen who settled in the community learned of work in this way. Furthermore, of those who settled there, nine first came to visit. Similarly, of sixty migrants of the outsider group interviewed in Wasco by Goldschmidt, thirty-two mentioned the presence of relatives as their reason for settling in the community, and forty stated that they had relatives in the town.

The movement of factory workers in the neighborhood clusters, and the influence of kin and neighbor on the direction of internal migration, point to the ways in which the movement of population takes

[2] Charles A. Myers and W. Rupert MacLaurin, *The Movement of Factory Workers* (New York, 1943), pp. 25–28.
[3] Walter Goldschmidt, *As You Sow* (New York, 1947), pp. 150–151.

place in aggregates, persistent in form for relatively longer and shorter periods, which in part account for the comparative isolation of these groups from one another. It is well known that the influence of friend and kin, and of the locality group, was highly determinant in the migration of the foreign-born. The many colonies of immigrants, the Little Italys, the Polish and the Irish settlements were often organized on a locality basis.

This is sufficient to indicate the nature of the group phenomenon of isolation resulting from the coming together of people of diverse origins and backgrounds and of differing interests. It is by and large a phenomenon of adjustment and is subject to change. Isolation in urban areas is nearly always reflected in variations in residential distribution of differing groups, and since this is so, measures of concentration and dispersion of distinguishable groups may be used to determine degrees of isolation.

We make a distinction between isolation and the segregation of groups. Segregation is the position of a group beyond a certain critical point of isolation, and is a tangible expression of systematic discrimination. Unlike the relative isolation of groups, forms of segregation change but slowly, since they find their support in the customary practices and the power system of the society as a whole.

DEGREES OF ISOLATION

The relative isolation of population groups may be measured by the ratio of their average percentages in the populations of neighborhoods where they live to their percentages in the total population of an area. If a group is randomly distributed, its average percentage in the populations of all the neighborhoods would equal its percentage in the population of the entire area; for this group the ratio would be 1.0. However, if a group is mainly concentrated in certain neighborhoods where its percentage in the population is much greater than its percentage in the population of the entire area, the ratio would be greater than 1.0. The ratio indicates the number of times the average concentration is greater than the group's percentage in the total population of the area studied, and is here taken as an index of isolation.[4]

Using census tracts as units for the measurement of group concentration, the index of isolation has been calculated in the following

---

[4] For other approaches to this problem, see Paul Hatt, "Spatial Patterns in a Polyethnic Area," *American Sociological Review*, 10 (1945), p. 355; and Julius Jahn, Calvin F. Schmid, and Clarence Schrag, "The Measurement of Ecological Segregation," *American Sociological Review*, 12 (1947), pp. 293–303.

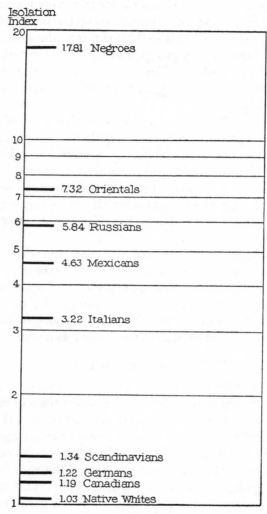

Fig. 13. Index of isolation.

manner for selected ethnic and foreign-born groups in Los Angeles County. The percentage of the population in each tract represented by each group was multiplied by the number of the group in that tract, and the sum of these products for all tracts was divided by the total number of the group in the county. This average percentage figure was divided by the percentage of the group in the county popu-

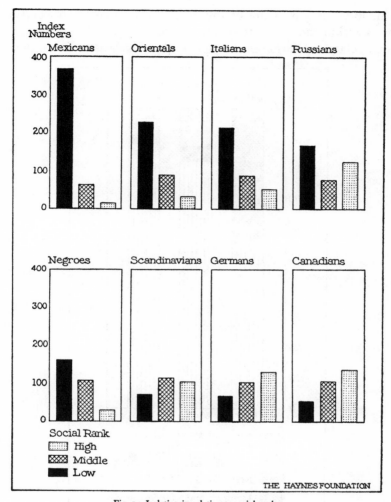

Fig. 14. Isolation in relation to social rank.

lation in order that the relative concentration of groups of varying size might be indicated.

$$\frac{\Sigma(P_1 N)/T}{P_2}$$

P_1— a group's percentage in the population of each census tract
N— the number of representatives of the group in each census tract
T— the total number of representatives of the group in Los Angeles County
P_2— the group's percentage in the population of Los Angeles County

This index is a measure of the extent of residential association of persons within the same group, and serves to place the several groups in their relative position on a single scale of isolation. The indexes of

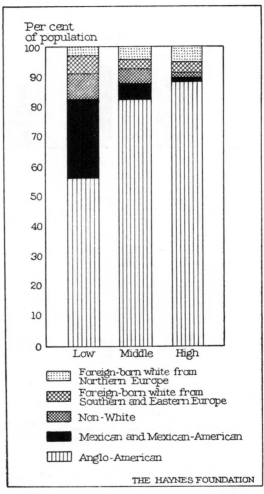

Fig. 15. Composition of the population at three levels of social rank.

isolation for selected groups are shown in figure 13. Five groups have indexes exceeding 3, meaning that their average concentration is three or more times what it would be if they were randomly distributed throughout the population of the county. These groups are the Negroes, Orientals, Russians (mainly Jewish), Mexicans, and Italians. The concentration of groups is differentially related to social rank. This is illustrated in figures 14 and 15. In figure 14, the percentage of the population at each level of rank represented by each group is expressed as an index number based on the group's percentage in the county as 100. The five most highly isolated groups show their greatest concentration at the low level of social rank, and, with the exception of the Russian group, show a decrease in percentage with increasing rank.

Figure 15 is presented as a summary of the population composition at each level of social rank. The grouping of the population varies from that used in figure 14, which does not include the total population. In figure 15, two groups, the Anglo-American and the foreign-born white from northern Europe, show an increasing percentage with increasing rank. Three groups, the Mexican, non-white, and foreign-born white from southern and eastern Europe, show a decreasing percentage with increasing rank.

SEGREGATION OF GROUPS

Far from being randomly distributed, these five groups, Negroes, Orientals, Russians (mainly Jewish), Mexicans, and Italians, are found in greater concentrations in some census tracts than in others, and they tend to be closely associated with one another in their distribution. Since the residential distribution of these highly isolated groups occurs in association with one another, this fact needs to be taken into account in the measurement of the degree of isolation in any one census tract. Not the concentration of single groups, but the total concentration of all the groups found in association, is the true measure of the degree of isolation under these conditions.

An index of the degree of isolation in each census tract may be provided by the percentage of the population represented by these five most highly concentrated groups. An index of 50 for a particular census tract means that 50 per cent of the population in the tract is composed of Negroes, Orientals, Mexicans, Russians, and Italians. Using this index for each census tract, the relative isolation of selected groups may be calculated. An average of the indexes for tracts in which a group is found was obtained through weighting each tract's index by the number of representatives of the group in the tract and dividing the sum of these products by the total number of the group

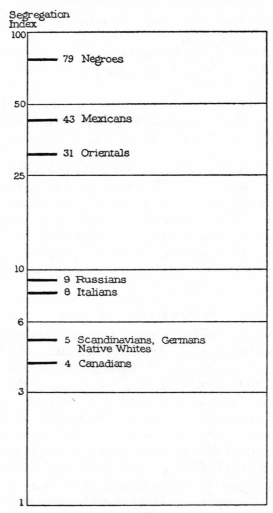

Fig. 16. Index of segregation.

in the county. The formula for measuring the degree of isolation for a group is thus modified to read:

$$\frac{\Sigma(P_3N)}{T}$$

P_3— the percentage of the population in each census tract represented by the five groups

N— the number of a particular group in each census tract

T— the total number of representatives of the particular group in Los Angeles County

Segregation has been distinguished from isolation as the position of a group beyond a critical point of isolation. The formula just described provides the basis for establishing this critical point, and is the index used here in the construction of an empirical scale of segregation which is presented in figure 16. On this scale the same five groups are set

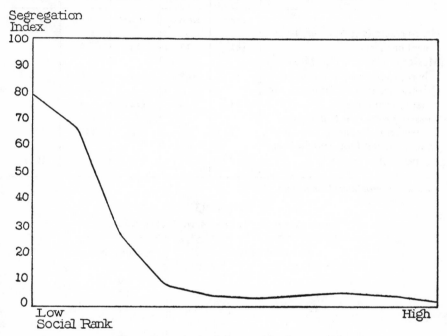

Fig. 17. Segregation in relation to social rank. $r = -50$.

apart from others, and significant differences in their segregation characteristics are also revealed.

Table 12, showing the residential interassociations of these five groups, will clarify the nature of the differences. The table shows the percentage of each group found in census tracts with the greatest concentrations of each of the other groups. The number of census tracts considered for each group, and therefore the area of concentration, was held approximately constant in order that the varying degrees of concentration might be comparable.

The position of the Negroes is highest on the first scale for isolation, and, since the association of both Mexicans and Orientals with them is relatively high, they occupy an extreme position on the scale of

TABLE 12

RESIDENTIAL ASSOCIATION OF FIVE ISOLATED GROUPS

(Figures indicate the percentage of each group living in the tracts indicated in the column on the left. Numbers in parentheses show the percentage of each group living in tracts of its highest concentration.)

Tracts	Negroes	Mexicans	Orientals	Russians	Italians
	per cent	*per cent*	*per cent*	*per cent*	*per cent*
Negro tracts (29; Negroes, 10 per cent or more)...............	(81)	13	14	2	4
Mexican tracts (32; Mexican-born, 10 per cent or more)......	10	(43)	17	6	12
Oriental tracts (33; Orientals, 10 per cent or more)............	11	13	(44)	4	5
Russian tracts (36; Russian-born, 3 per cent or more)...........	2	13	8	(52)	7
Italian tracts (30; Italian-born, 2 per cent or more)...........	1	15	5	3	(29)

SOURCE: United States Census, 1940.

TABLE 13

SEGREGATION IN RELATION TO SOCIAL RANK

Social-rank deciles	Segregation index
Low: 1........................	79
2........................	67
3........................	26
Middle: 4........................	8
5........................	4
6........................	3
High: 7........................	4
8........................	5
9........................	4
10.......................	2

SOURCE: United States Census, 1940.

segregation. Thirteen per cent of all Mexicans and 14 per cent of Orientals live in the twenty-nine tracts where Negro concentration is greatest. The isolation index for Orientals is higher than that for Mexicans, but the position of the two groups is reversed for the segregation index since three groups, Negroes, Orientals, and Italians, have

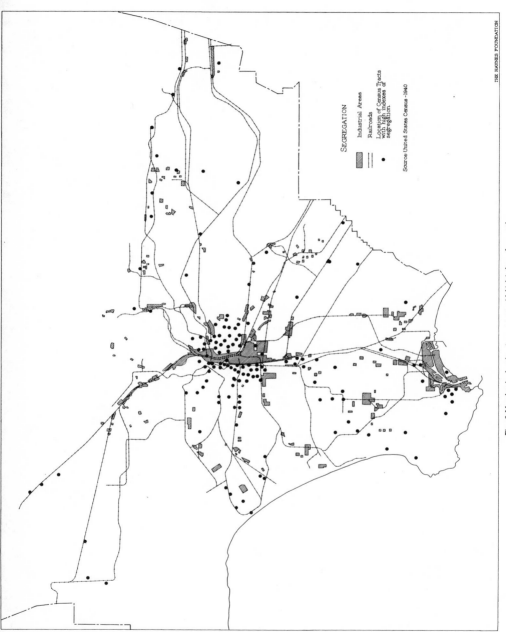

SEGREGATION

Industrial Areas

Railroads

Location of Census Tracts
with high indexes of
segregation.

Source United States Census –1940

Fig. 18. Map showing location of census tracts with high indexes of segregation.

marked associations with the Mexicans, but only two groups, Negroes and Mexicans, are associated with the Orientals. The indexes of isolation for the Russians and the Italians are among the highest, but their indexes of segregation are low since only one other group, the Mexicans, has over 10 per cent of its population living in the neighborhoods where they are concentrated.

It was pointed out earlier that isolation of groups is differentially related to social rank, and that the five most isolated groups are largely concentrated in the lowest level. Segregation as operationally defined in this discussion is likewise definitely associated with the low level of rank. This association is described in table 13 and figure 17. Table 13 gives the median indexes of segregation for census tracts in each decile of the range of social rank. Figure 17 illustrates this trend.

The location of census tracts, 146 in number, with indexes of segregation above the average for the county, is shown in figure 18. All census tracts with indexes of 14 or over are included.

PART TWO

SOCIAL AREAS OF LOS ANGELES

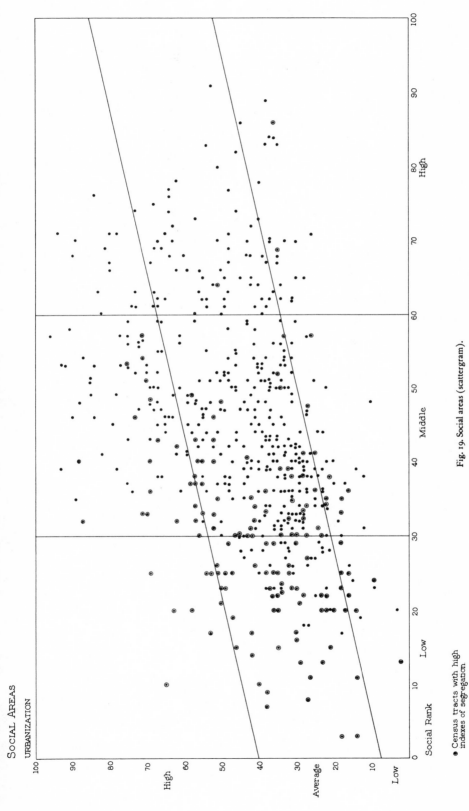

SOCIAL AREAS

URBANIZATION

Social Rank

Low · · · · Middle · · · · High

Fig. 19. Social areas (scattergram).

● Census tracts with high
indexes of segregation

VI. Elements of an Urban Typology

BASIC TO our approach in this study of the population of Los Angeles has been the concept of social position. Applying this concept to populations rather than to individuals and, therefore, taking census tracts as our units, we have determined the position of population groups on the basis of three modes of differentiation. On one scale we measured the standing of the population in each census tract in an order of social rank. On a second scale we measured the degree of urbanization. In a diagram of urban society the position of one population group in relation to all other population groups may be determined, as a first approximation, on the basis of these two scores within a two-dimensional space. In figure 19 the position of each of the 570-odd census tracts has been plotted with reference to these two scales. It is observed, however, that a third element has to be taken into account before the social position of populations can be determined adequately. The presence of certain distinguishable population groups in concentrations vastly exceeding their concentration in the total population necessitates the introduction of a distinction to be made on this basis. This distinction is the third dimension of the urban social space as we conceive it. In figure 19 this distinction is made by encircling tracts with high concentrations of these groups. These tracts have segregation indexes above the average for the county, 14 or over.

The way in which we deal with complex data of this sort in daily life, and the empirical procedures used in scientific study, have certain features in common. Our interest is in modal rather than in extreme characteristics, and both in daily life and in scientific study we seek to summarize our observations by constructs that we call types. In the impersonal setting of the city, for example, social standing does not rest on any intimate evaluation of persons, nor any discriminating appraisal of differences within groups. Instead, certain easily recognizable traits, such as houses and possessions, become symbolic of rank.

In urban-industrial society the unfailing indicators of the social position of others readily accessible to everyone are houses and areas of residence. As every occupation is evaluated and generally accorded honor and esteem on a scale of prestige in society, so every residential section has a status value which is readily recognized by everyone in the city. Even a casual visitor in Los Angeles could name half a dozen places representative of the exclusive sections on the west side and along the foothills of the Santa Monica and San Gabriel mountains. Such places as Brentwood, Westwood, Beverly Hills, Flintridge, and San Marino will readily come to mind. Someone more familiar with the city could name Bunker Hill, Belvedere, Pacoima, and Watts as representative of sections at the other end of the scale.

In this setting, whether we operate on the basis of common sense or go about our task systematically, following the method of science, an underlying tendency of our minds is a belief in the existence of broad regularities in social phenomena. It is this tendency of our minds that enables us to select certain traits, certain items of behavior, and items in external characteristics, out of the multitude of traits and characteristics we observe about persons or places, and to summarize them in shorthand fashion. These we recognize as types, and we make generalizations about our observations on the basis of our recognition of these types.

No matter at what level of abstraction we operate in social analysis, if our findings are to have any value superior to that of uncontrolled common sense, we need to follow the method of science and attempt to isolate and abstract the relevant and recurrent elements and study the orderly relations that exist among them. This is the main purpose of this section on classification and typology, as it has been the chief emphasis of our approach to the study of urban society in Los Angeles. Morris R. Cohen, in discussing type analysis as a method of science,[1] points out that "procedures that begin with the study of types follow the order of learning in daily life." For we know that, in daily life also, whenever we think of a cluster of attributes we inevitably use the concept of type. This is the way our minds work. In memory we select this or that characteristic, throw into relief some special combination of attributes. Our language is full of terms that are nothing but labels of types. Even stereotypes in terms of which we think about people are constructs of this sort.

Study of types as a method of science is not only a way of following the order of learning in daily life; it is made necessary by certain other considerations as well. In systematic social inquiry the need of obtaining a rounded picture of life in any detail places a limit on the field of

[1] *Reason and Nature: An Essay on the Meaning of the Scientific Method* (New York, 1931), p. 365.

observation. We cannot study every city or every population grouping in it, any more than we can study any one city or group with respect to every detail of social life. There must be choice and emphasis. Out of this necessity in the laying out of comparative work in sociology there has arisen what has been termed "cultural taxonomy," which is simply the problem of the recognition of types and the identification of single population groupings as examples of these types. When types are established, a single sample may be selected to represent a category, a class of population groupings.[2]

As long ago as the middle of the nineteenth century, Adolphe Quetelet contended that social sciences must in large measure be concerned with the determination of types.[3] This is the objective of the scientific study of the city as we see it. It is for this reason that so large a proportion of this discussion has dealt with method and principle, and with an attempt at a classification of the distinctive features of urban life. In the absence of such definitions and an understanding of the nature of general relationships it would be useless to introduce material descriptive of urban problems that are compounded of general impressions and uncontrolled observation. Even the use of statistical data, in the absence of such clarification of the field, is bound to be misleading and will only add to the confusion that exists in our minds about the problems of the city.

SOCIAL AREAS AS TYPES

A type is a cluster of mutually dependent attributes considered as a whole. It may be constructed out of primary data. Thus established empirically, it serves as a summary of our observations, and a way of perceiving order in complexity. In the comparative study of groups a type may be taken as representative of a category, of a general class of population groupings under observation.

In recent years, Paul Lazarsfeld, both in his researches and in his discussions of method, has done much to clarify the nature of the empirical procedures used in the establishment of types.[4] At a level of generalization where several attributes are taken into account in the manner indicated here, Lazarsfeld has introduced the concept of attribute space. We have adopted this concept in the organization of

[2] For a lucid statement of this problem, see the discussion of method in Hsiao-T'ung Fei and Chih-I Chang, *Earthbound China: A Study of Rural Economy in Yunnan* (Chicago, 1944), pp. 13–16.

[3] Lambert Adolphe Jacques Quetelet, *Du système social et des lois qui le régissent* (Paris, 1848).

[4] See Paul F. Lazarsfeld, "Some Remarks on the Typological Procedures in Social Research," *Zeitschrift für Sozialforschung*, 6 (1937), pp. 119–139.

our material. In order to group census tracts with similar indexes for social rank, urbanization, and segregation, a three-dimensional attribute space was, therefore, conceived. Census tracts were placed first in a two-dimensional attribute space, with the index of urbanization related to the base, social rank. The base was divided into three intervals of approximate thirds of the range, indicating low, middle,

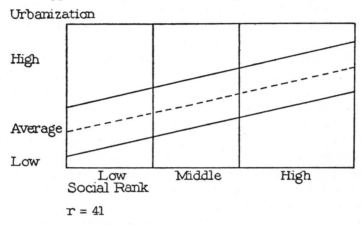

$r = 41$

and high social rank. The index of urbanization was divided into three intervals, with the middle or average interval determined by the space of two standard errors about the regression line of urbanization

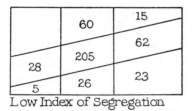

Low Index of Segregation

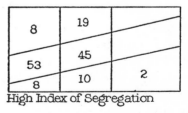

High Index of Segregation

related to social rank. The third dimension was added to this attribute space by dividing the census tracts in each area into two parts according to their indexes of segregation. Indexes at the average or above, 14 and over, were considered high, and those below the average, low. Census tracts are distributed in 16 of the possible 18 resulting social areas in the manner illustrated by the accompanying figures.

The distribution of the population by social areas is given in figure 20. When the population is considered without distinction between census tracts with high and low indexes of segregation, most of the

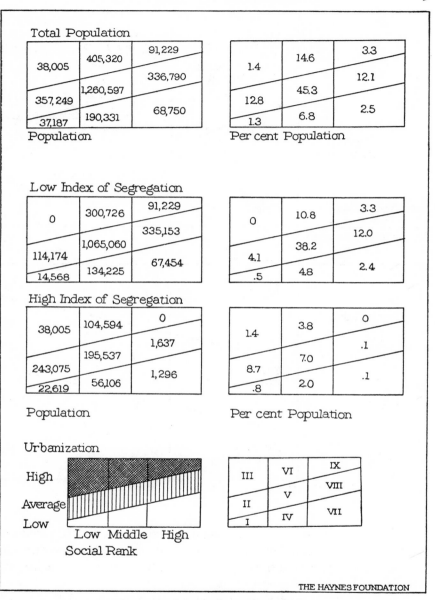

Fig. 20. Population distribution by social areas.

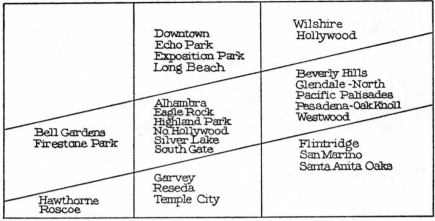

Low Index of Segregation

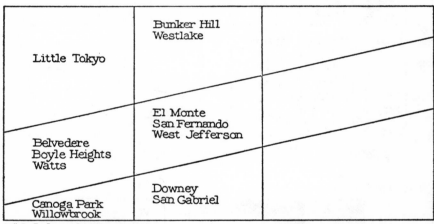

High Index of Segregation

Fig. 21. Selected places representative of social areas.

population is within the middle range of social rank and the average range of urbanization. The modes of both distributions are within the central area indicated in the key to the diagram as area V. The largest population is concentrated in this area.

When census tracts with low indexes of segregation are distinguished from those with high indexes, differences in the distribution of population are revealed. This distribution emphasizes the fact that segregation is mainly associated with the low level of social rank. The

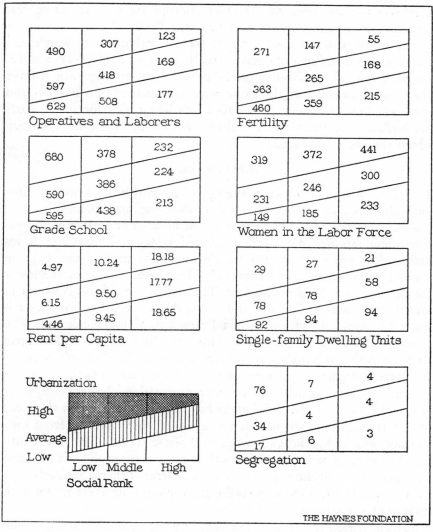

Fig. 22. Median ratios for social areas.

percentage of the total population with low social rank is proportionately greater in census tracts with high indexes of segregation than in tracts with low indexes.

In figure 21, names of places representative of social areas are given. Median ratios for the areas are shown in figure 22. The median has been selected and used as the most appropriate measure of central tendency in the description of social areas.

The mean was not used, since it was desirable not to weight extreme variations. Since the census tracts in areas I, III, VII, and IX are very few, the reliability of the mode as an average would have been questionable. For the same reason, measures of variation and skewness have not been introduced. Median ratios for social areas are included for the seven variables used in the three indexes upon which the areas are based.

SOCIAL RANK

The index of social rank is an average of the percentile scores of three variables: level of occupation, level of schooling, and income.

Level of occupation.—Measured by the number of craftsmen, operatives, and laborers per 1,000 employed persons. The actual ratios rather than percentile scores are shown in the part of the diagram labeled "Operatives and Laborers." The higher the ratio, the lower the occupational level of the area. The occupational level is lowest in area I, with low social rank and a low degree of urbanization. It is highest in area IX, with high social rank and high urbanization. The trend at each level of social rank is toward a higher occupational level with increasing urbanization. The trend at each level of urbanization is toward a higher occupation level with higher social rank.

Since the level of urbanization increases with each increasing level of social rank, and the social areas have been delineated on the basis of this trend, the ratios for each level of urbanization represent low, average, and high, relative to each level of social rank. The ratios indicated at average urbanization are the averages for each level of social rank since most of the population is concentrated there. Similarly, the ratios given at the middle level of social rank are the averages for each level of urbanization.

Level of schooling.—This is measured by the number of persons who had completed grade school or less per 1,000 persons twenty-five years old and over. The actual ratios are shown in the diagram and labeled "Grade School." Again, the higher the ratio, the lower the level of schooling. The level of schooling is lowest in area III, where urbanization is high and social rank is low and where all the census tracts have high indexes of segregation. The level of schooling is highest in area VII, where urbanization is low, social rank is high, and where all the census tracts have low indexes of segregation. The trend at each level of urbanization is toward a higher level of schooling with increasing social rank. The general trend at the low and high levels of social rank is toward a lower level of schooling with increasing urbanization, but, within the middle range of social rank, the trend is toward higher level of schooling with increasing urbanization.

Rent as a measure of income.—The third variable in the index of social rank is a measure of income, rent per capita, the average rent related to the population. Average rent per capita is given for each social area. Inferences about the income characteristics of social areas are presented elsewhere in this section.

URBANIZATION

The index of urbanization is an average of the percentile scores of three variables: fertility, women in the labor force, and single-family dwelling units.

Fertility.—Measured by the number of children under five per 1,000 women 15–44. The higher the ratio, the higher the fertility of an area. The highest fertility is in area I, with low social rank and low urbanization, while the lowest ratio is in area IX, with high social rank and high urbanization. Fertility decreases with increasing social rank and with increasing urbanization.

Women in the labor force.—The second variable in the index of urbanization is the number of women in the labor force per 1,000 women of fourteen years and over. The percentage of women in paid employment increases with urbanization and with social rank. The highest percentage is in area IX, with high urbanization and high social rank. The lowest percentage is in area I, with low urbanization and low social rank.

Single-family dwelling units.—The percentage of occupied dwelling units which are single-family detached is the third variable in the index of urbanization. The percentages for each area are indicated.

SEGREGATION

The average index of segregation for each social area is the percentage of the population represented by the five most highly isolated groups. Again, the association of segregation with the low level of social rank is emphasized. In area III, where all the census tracts have indexes above the average for the county, the average index of segregation is highest. In area VII, where none of the tracts have indexes above the average for the county, the average index is lowest. At each level of urbanization, the index at the low level of social rank is highest.

TABLE 14

IDENTIFYING PLACE NAMES FOR REPRESENTATIVE TRACTS BY SOCIAL RANK AND GROUP PREDOMINANCE, 1940

Predominant group	Social rank		
	Low	Middle	High
Mexicans............	*53 tracts* Azusa Belvedere Boyle Heights Canoga Park Chavez Ravine Lincoln Heights Pacoima Watts	*40 tracts* Duarte El Monte Irwindale Los Nietos Puente San Fernando San Gabriel	.. ..
Orientals...........	*10 tracts* Hawthorne Little Tokyo Sawtelle Terminal Island Torrance Willowbrook	*12 tracts* Gardena Downtown Pico-Vermont	.. ..
Negroes............	*4 tracts* Watts	*19 tracts* Central Avenue Pasadena—Lincoln Avenue West Jefferson	.. .. ..
Russians...........	*2 tracts* Boyle Heights	*3 tracts* Beverly-Fairfax West Adams	.. ..

SOURCE: United States Census, 1940.

SEGREGATED GROUP DIFFERENTIALS

Our entire procedure in the setting up of social areas and the identification of social areas as types rests on the recognition of three kinds of differences as basic to the creation of social distinctions among urban

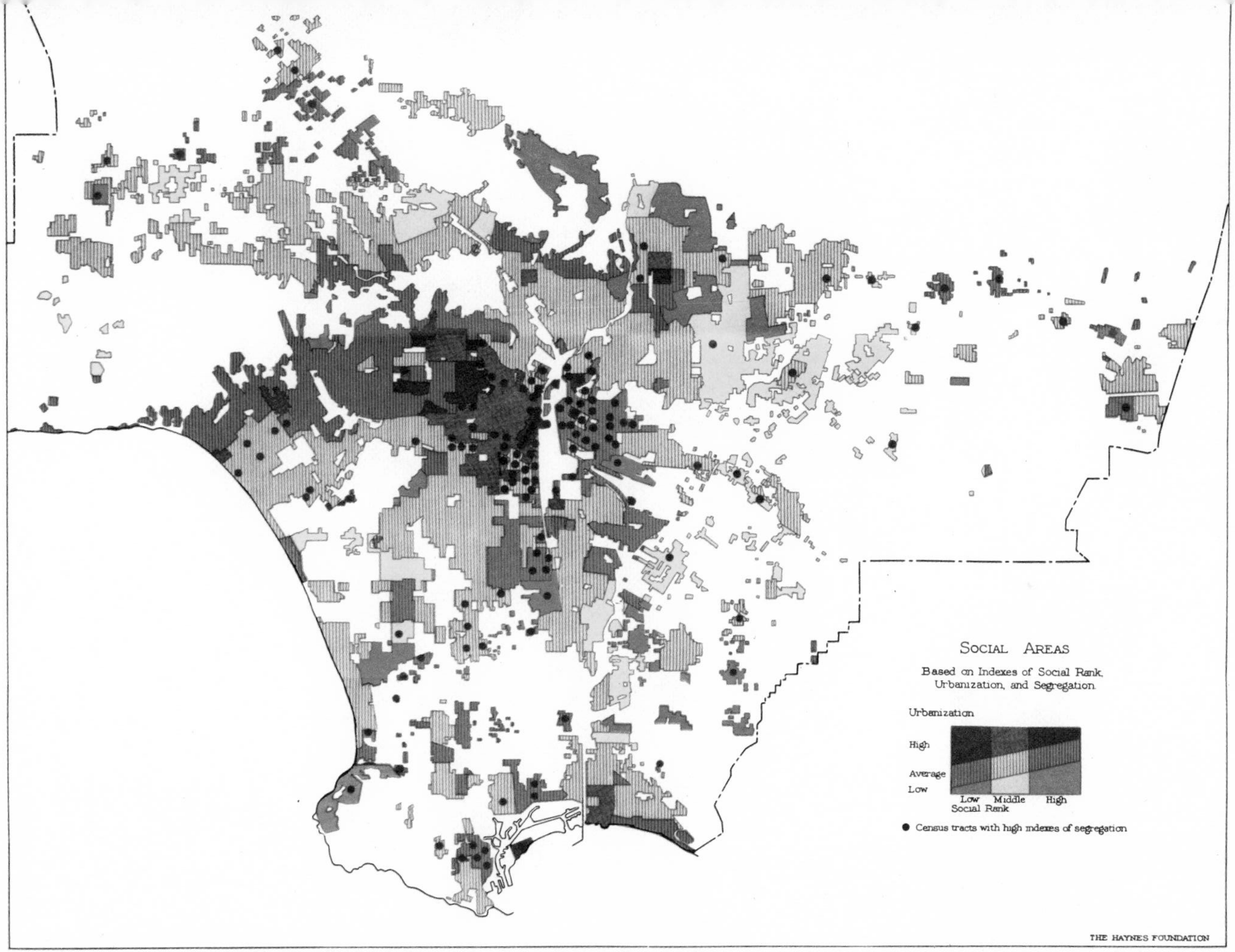

SOCIAL AREAS

Based on Indexes of Social Rank,
Urbanization, and Segregation.

Urbanization

High
Average
Low

Low   Middle   High
Social Rank

● Census tracts with high indexes of segregation.

Fig. 23. Map showing social areas.

populations. These differences are (1) differences in social rank, (2) differences in urbanization, and (3) differences in the degree of segregation. We have shown that these differences among populations occur as variations that are graded and measurable. In the actual development of our procedure, we have determined the social position of

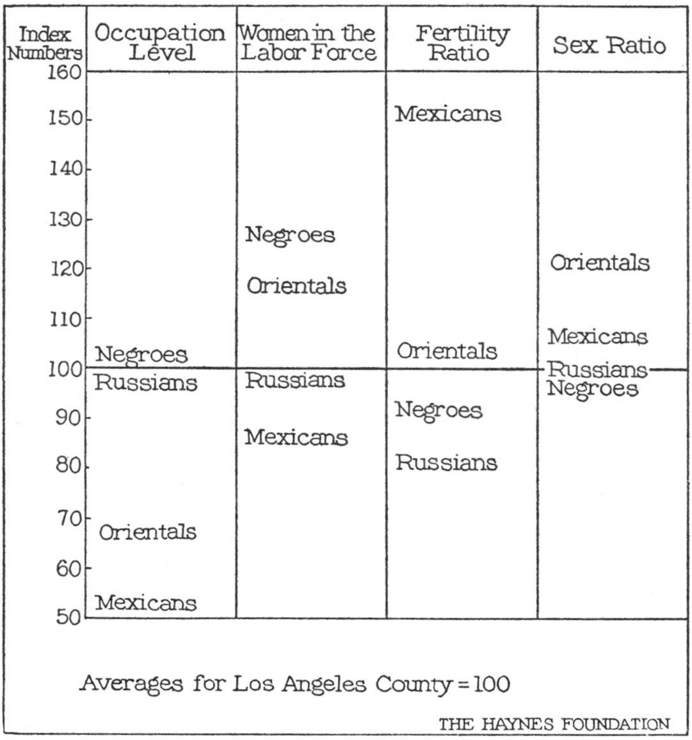

Index Numbers	Occupation Level	Women in the Labor Force	Fertility Ratio	Sex Ratio
160				
150			Mexicans	
140				
130		Negroes		
120		Orientals		Orientals
110				
100	Negroes		Orientals	Mexicans
	Russians	Russians		Russians Negroes
90		Mexicans	Negroes	
80			Russians	
70	Orientals			
60				
50	Mexicans			

Averages for Los Angeles County = 100

THE HAYNES FOUNDATION

Fig. 24. Variations in group characteristics.

populations, first, within the coördinates of the two variables, social rank and urbanization. The grouping of populations falling into the approximate thirds of the range of variation in social rank and urbanization has enabled us to identify nine basic social areas or population types.

It would have been possible, by means of a similar handling of the third variable, segregation, to arrive at a much larger number of types. It was preferable, however, to keep the organization of the material as simple as possible, since the comparative treatment of a multiplicity of types in any detail would have been unwieldy and unnecessarily complicated. In the actual treatment of the variable, segregation, therefore, the census tracts, rather than being arranged in a graded series, were instead divided into two simple categories characterized by indexes of high and low segregation. All census tracts with indexes above the average for the county were placed in the first category; census tracts with indexes below the average for the county were placed in the second category.

Here it is necessary to return, then, to a consideration of some of the more important differentials among segregated groups. Chief among these differentials are the differentials in social rank. Populations of 69 tracts, constituting 47 per cent of those with high indexes, are at the low level of social rank. Mexicans are predominant in 53 of these tracts, Orientals in 10, Negroes in 4, and Russians in 2. Seventy-four tracts, 51 per cent, are at the middle level. Mexicans are predominant in 40, Negroes in 19, Orientals in 12, and Russians in 3. Only three tracts with very small populations are at the high level of social rank. In contrast with this distribution, only 8 per cent of tracts with low indexes of segregation are at the low level of rank, 69 per cent at the middle level, and 23 per cent at the high level.

	Percentage of census tracts at three levels of social rank		
	Low	*Middle*	*High*
Tracts with low indexes of segregation...................	8	69	23
Tracts with high indexes of segregation...................	47	51	2

Table 14 gives the identifying names of selected census tracts classified by social rank and group predominance. Mexicans are the most predominant group in 95 tracts, Negroes in 23, Orientals in 23, and Russians in 5.

A diagrammatic representation of variations in group characteristics is shown in figure 24. In the construction of this diagram, median ratios for selected social factors were calculated for each group, choosing in each case specific tracts in which there was a numerical preponderance of the group considered. The 95 tracts in which Mexicans predominate were used to determine the median ratios for Mexicans. The 23 tracts in which Negroes predominate were used in calculating the ratios for Negroes. Similarly, ratios for Orientals and Russians were based only on the tracts where they predominate. Since data are not available for each group separately for each of the characteristics selected, this method was used in order that the medians derived

Area	Mexicans	Orientals	Negroes	Italians	Russians	Total Population
I	2.8	1.9	1.4	.9	.3	1.3
II	43.4	19.9	20.1	25.5	25.3	12.8
III	5.9	13.1	3.2	6.4	.4	1.4
IV	7.4	5.9	.9	3.9	1.4	6.8
V	28.0	31.8	49.8	43.3	30.4	45.2
VI	10.2	21.5	19.3	11.1	19.9	14.6
VII	4	.8	.5	1.0	.6	2.5
VIII	1.6	3.7	4.4	6.2	15.1	12.1
IX	.3	1.4	.4	1.7	6.6	3.3
	100.0	100.0	100.0	100.0	100.0	100.0

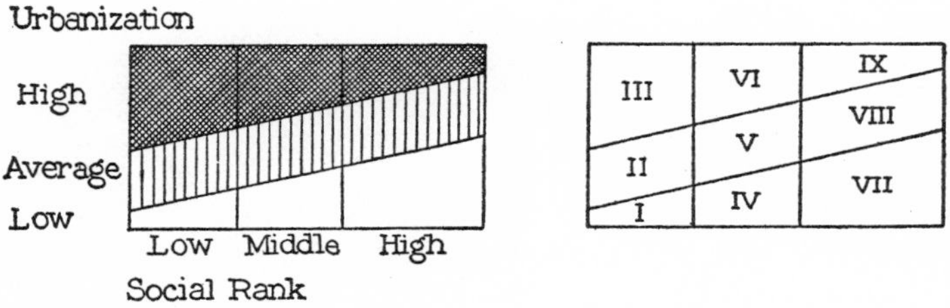

THE HAYNES FOUNDATION

Fig. 25. Distribution of groups in social areas.

should be as nearly as possible representative of the characteristics of each group. The ratios were converted to index numbers based on the averages for each ratio for the county. The relative position of each group for each characteristic is shown in figure 24. The occupation levels of the Negro and of the Russian populations are around the average for the county. Negroes and Orientals have a higher proportion of

women in the labor force than the other groups. Mexicans have highest
fertility, Russians lowest. The proportion of men is greatest for Orientals and least for Negroes.

These variations in group characteristics are basic among factors
making for social distinctions among groups. These social distinctions
find their expression in the differential distribution of groups in social
areas. The form of this distribution is shown in figure 25. In the construction of this diagram, data from all census tracts were used. The
percentage of each of the five groups in each social area, and the percentage distribution of the total population, are given in the diagram.
In comparison with the total population, Mexicans have a higher
proportion of their group in areas I–IV, and a lower proportion in
areas V–IX. Orientals have a higher proportion in areas I, II, III,
and VI and a lower proportion in the others. Negroes have a higher
proportion in areas I, II, III, V, and VI; Italians, in areas II and III;
and Russians, in areas II, VI, and VIII.

VII. Some Generalizations

GENERALIZATIONS ABOUT AGE STRUCTURE AND THE SEX RATIO

THREE broad generalizations may be made about the age structure of human populations. First, in all large human populations there is a remarkable stability in the proportion of the total

TABLE 15

AGE STRUCTURE OF VARIOUS POPULATIONS AT SPECIFIED DATES

Country	Year	Age group		
		0–14	15–49	50+
		per cent	*per cent*	*per cent*
Brazil.................	1920	42.7	48.3	8.9
Turkey................	1935	41.3	45.5	13.2
India.................	1931	39.9	50.4	9.7
Mexico................	1930	39.2	50.2	10.6
U.S.S.R...............	1926	37.2	49.9	13.1
Bulgaria..............	1934	35.6	49.2	15.2
Canada...............	1931	31.7	51.6	16.6
Italy.................	1931	29.7	50.9	19.4
United States.........	1930	29.4	53.4	17.3
Irish Free State........	1926	29.2	48.4	22.4
Australia..............	1921	27.5	53.3	19.1
New Zealand..........	1936	25.5	52.7	21.8
Germany..............	1933	24.2	54.0	21.8
England and Wales.....	1931	23.8	53.4	22.8
Belgium..............	1930	22.9	54.2	22.9
France................	1931	22.9	51.9	25.7
Sweden...............	1935	22.2	54.4	23.4

SOURCE: Raymond Pearl, "Aging of Populations," *Journal of the American Statistical Association,* 35 (1940), table 1, p. 282.

population between the ages of fifteen and forty-nine; second, the greatest variation among human groups occurs in the proportion of the population under fifteen years of age; third, the proportion of the population past fifty years of age varies in general in a compensatory way with the variation in the proportion of the young.

Students of the biology of human populations have repeatedly pointed out that the age distribution of living populations has far more than a merely statistical interest. Variations in the proportions of the young, the mature, and the old find their expression in all

TABLE 16
AGE STRUCTURE OF THE POPULATION IN VARIOUS STATES, 1940

State	Age group		
	0–14	15–49	50+
	per cent	*per cent*	*per cent*
New Mexico........................	34.5	51.6	13.9
Mississippi........................	32.6	52.1	15.2
North Carolina....................	32.5	53.7	13.8
Georgia...........................	30.8	53.3	15.9
Louisiana.........................	29.7	54.7	15.5
Oklahoma.........................	29.2	52.9	17.8
Texas............................	28.0	55.4	16.6
Maine............................	26.1	49.9	24.0
Vermont..........................	25.8	49.9	24.3
Iowa.............................	24.6	51.7	23.7
Pennsylvania......................	24.2	55.0	20.8
Ohio.............................	22.9	54.4	22.7
Massachusetts.....................	21.8	54.2	24.0
Illinois...........................	21.6	56.2	22.1
Washington.......................	21.1	54.0	24.9
New York.........................	20.6	57.5	21.9
California.........................	19.8	56.1	24.1

SOURCE: United States Census, 1940.

human groupings in the reproductive capacity and the work capacity of the population as a whole. We may express this relationship as the balance of workers and consumers in groups, and we find that the balance is profoundly influenced by the technology and the resource organization in society.

It appears that first to appreciate the significance of these broad regularities in the age structure of populations was the Swedish statistician Sundbärg.[1] On the basis of a comparative study of a number of populations, Sundbärg concluded that in a population unaffected by migration the mature group, those between the ages of fifteen and

[1] A. G. Sundbärg, Institut International de Statistique, *Bulletin*, 12 (1900), pp. 90–95.

forty-nine, constituted approximately 50 per cent of the total. He proposed a classification of human populations which depended on the preponderance of the young or the old in relation to those in the reproductive ages.

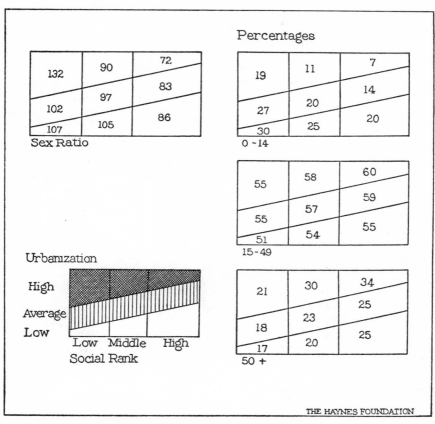

Fig. 26. Age and sex characteristics of social areas.

Following the lead of Sundbärg, Raymond Pearl published in 1930,[2] and again in 1940,[3] statistics on the distribution of the populations of a number of countries according to the threefold division of the human life cycle. More recently, Rupert Vance[4] applied this type of analysis to the population of the United States, made some modifications in

[2] "Some Aspects of the Biology of Human Populations," in E. V. Cowdry, *Human Biology and Racial Welfare* (New York, 1930), pp. 521–525.
[3] "The Aging of Populations," *Journal of the American Statistical Association*, 35 (1940), pp. 280–283.
[4] *All These People* (Chapel Hill, 1946), pp. 48–61.

the classification, and drew inferences from it concerning the human resources of the South.

Tables 15 and 16 present data on the distribution of various populations in different countries and states in these three broad groups of youth, maturity, and old age.

TABLE 17

AGE STRUCTURE OF VARIOUS POPULATIONS IN LOS ANGELES COUNTY, 1940

Social area	Identifying place name	Age group			Sex ratio
		0–14	15–49	50+	
		per cent	*per cent*	*per cent*	
I	Hawthorne..................	31.8	51.2	17.0	112
	Canoga Park................	30.6	50.1	19.3	104
II	Belvedere Gardens...........	27.2	53.3	19.5	99
	Boyle Heights...............	27.0	54.6	18.4	98
IV	San Gabriel.................	25.6	55.5	18.9	98
	Lamanda Park..............	25.0	55.5	19.5	94
III	Little Tokyo................	22.8	55.7	21.5	149
V	Leimert....................	19.9	60.8	19.3	89
	Sierra Madre...............	19.4	45.9	34.7	87
VII	Altadena...................	17.8	52.6	29.6	84
	Pasadena—East Orange Grove..	16.5	51.2	32.3	81
VIII	Westwood..................	16.2	61.9	21.9	76
	Beverly Hills...............	13.7	61.0	25.3	72
VI	Westlake...................	10.6	55.7	33.7	76
	Long Beach—Central.........	8.4	43.0	48.6	75
IX	Hollywood—Central..........	6.1	57.6	36.3	77
	Wilshire...................	3.6	54.9	41.5	60

SOURCE: United States Census, 1940.

Vance, in applying Sundbärg's classification to the American population, pointed to the difficulty of setting up age limits for a mature group that will include both the productive and the reproductive functions.[5] Sundbärg, by delimiting maturity between ages fifteen to forty-nine, came near a grouping that fitted the biologic conditions of reproduction, but hardly the economic and cultural functions of mature populations in a technologically advanced society.

Table 17 presents data on the distribution of various populations in Los Angeles in these three broad groups of youth, maturity, and old

[5] *Ibid.*, p. 48.

Sex Ratio

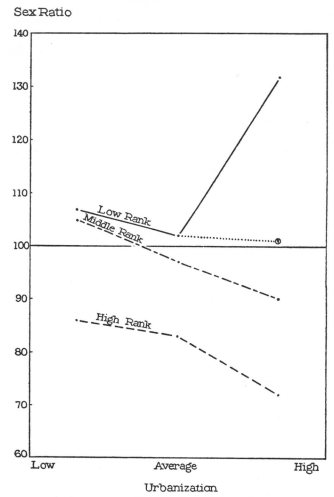

Fig. 27. Median sex ratios at three levels of urbanization for each of the three levels of social rank. Circled dot: possible ratio for low social rank at high urbanization.

age. Figure 26 describes the age characteristics of social areas on the basis of this threefold classification. The variations in the sex ratio associated with this pattern of age distribution are also shown in the chart.

There are more men than women in populations at the lower levels of rank, and more women than men in populations at the higher levels, since the sex ratio is highest at the lowest levels and declines with increasing rank. There are more men than women in populations at low levels of urbanization, except in populations at the highest level of rank. The proportion of women in the total population increases with increasing urbanization, except at the lowest level of rank, where high urbanization coincides with the highest sex ratios.

The increasing proportion of women in the total population with increasing social rank and increasing urbanization is further described in figure 27, where median sex ratios at three levels of urbanization for each of the three levels of social rank are given. In social area III, where the median sex ratio is above 130, the enormous concentration of men in certain populations is associated with low-level occupations. In this social area a single population group in census tract 72 has a sex ratio of 92, which is below the average for the county that stands at 96. This is an established population in one of the older sections of the city, and is now declining in numbers.

The presence of this population at the low level of rank with high urbanization suggests a possible state of affairs in which the sex ratio at low rank may be found to conform to the trend at other levels and decline with increasing urbanization. This possible ratio is indicated as a hypothetical point on the diagram.

A generalized summary of the data on the variations of the sex ratio in the total population is presented in figure 28, where a twofold division of the population is shown. In this scattergram, which (except only in shapes of dots) is the same as the one introduced at the beginning of the section dealing with urban typology, census tracts with sex ratios above the ratio for the county, 97 and above, are shown as solid circles; census tracts with sex ratios below the ratio for the county are shown as hollow circles. This twofold division of the population points to the basis of one of the more important differentials in urban society. The two segments in the diagram stand for the two extreme positions of the urban world.

In a preliminary classification of the population of Los Angeles on the basis of this generalized description of the age structure and the sex ratio, the social areas fall within two broad categories, the characteristics of which are as follows.

One broad group includes the social areas in which there are large numbers of children in relation to the total population, a higher proportion of youth, a lower proportion in working ages, and, relative to the county as a whole, fewer older-age persons. Social areas I–V are

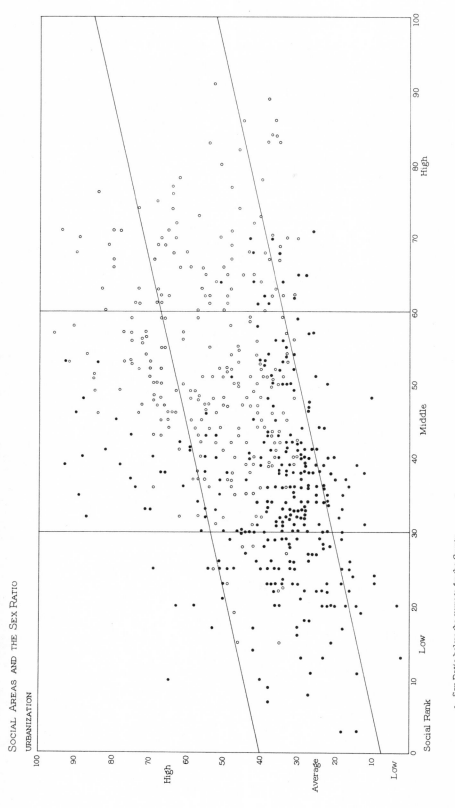

SOCIAL AREAS AND THE SEX RATIO

URBANIZATION

Fig. 28. Social areas and the sex ratio.

○ Sex Ratio below the average for the County
● Sex Ratio above the average for the County

	More Men Than Women		More Women Than Men	
Age Structure	More children Higher proportion of youth Lower proportion in working ages Fewer old age I - V		Fewer children Lower proportion of youth Higher proportion in working ages Higher proportion of old age VI - IX	
Occupation Level	High Segregation	Low Segregation	High Segregation	Low Segregation
10 9 Higher managerial, Higher professional 8				IX VIII VII
Professional Lower managerial, 7 Higher White collar 6				VI
Lower managerial, Lower 5 professional, White collar 4		V	VI	
White collar, 3 Services, Skilled craft 2	IV, V III	IV		
1 Skilled factory, Unskilled 0	II I	I, II		

Fig. 29. Classification of social areas based on age, sex, and occupation level.

of this group. These areas have higher sex ratios than the average for the county. The second broad group includes the social areas in which there are fewer children, a lower proportion of youth, higher proportion in working ages, and higher proportion of old age. Social areas VI–IX fall within this group. These social areas have sex ratios uniformly lower than the average for the county.

The classification of the social areas of Los Angeles into these two broad categories is shown in figure 29 in relation to levels of occupation. The scale for occupation level is based on the range of median occupation ratios for social areas. Occupations characteristic of each level are designated by name in relation to the scale.

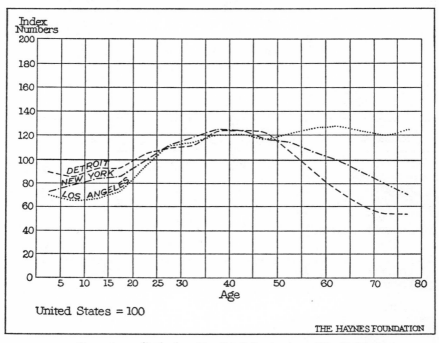

Fig. 30. Age profiles for three cities: Detroit, Los Angeles, and New York.

AGE PROFILE OF POPULATIONS

The detailed examination of the age structure of representative populations by social areas, and their comparison with one another, is facilitated by the use of index numbers and the construction of age profiles based on them.[6]

Figure 30 gives the age profiles of three cities, Los Angeles, New York, and Detroit, in relation to a base of 100 in the United States. The percentage of the population in each age group for the three cities

[6] See T. Lynn Smith, "Some Aspects of Village Demography," *Social Forces*, 20 (1941), pp. 15–25. For an application of this type of analysis to regional data, see his *Brazil: People and Institutions* (Louisiana State University Press, 1946), pp. 200–211.

is expressed as a percentage of the figures for the United States. Figures 31 and 32 show the age profiles of representative populations in the Los Angeles area in relation to a base of 100 in the county as a whole.

Predominance of persons in the working ages is typical of all cities. This concentration of younger adults and of persons in the middle

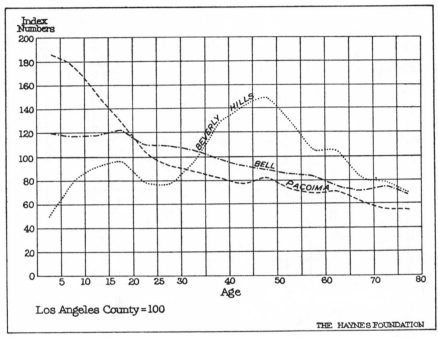

Fig. 31. Age profiles for Beverly Hills, Bell, and Pacoima (Los Angeles County census tracts 381, 505, and 4).

years of life in cities gives the age profile of urban populations its characteristic form, sharply differentiating it from the age profile of rural populations, where an excess of children and a relatively low proportion of persons in old age is associated with deficiency of persons in the productive years of life. Cities differ from one another, however, in the relative importance of youth and old age in their total population.

Each of the three age profiles in figure 30 represents a variation of the age structure characteristic of urban populations in general. The selective migration of persons in the productive years of life accounts for the preponderance of those age groups in all three cities. Regional differences in the fertility of populations account for the variations in the proportion of the child population. Selective migration of persons in older ages plus the differences in the proportion of younger people account for the variations in the proportion of the old.

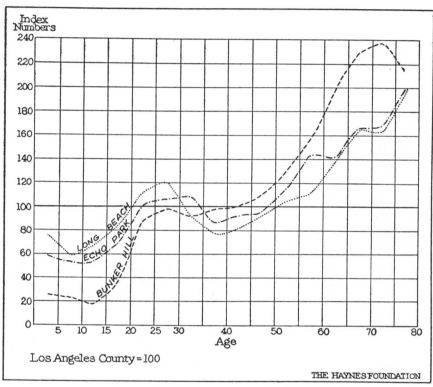

Fig. 32. Age profiles for Long Beach, Echo Park, and Bunker Hill (Los Angeles County census tracts 313, 114, and 181).

Within each city, the age structure of the population varies more widely. The profiles in figure 31 illustrate one aspect of the variation. These profiles range from a type usually encountered in the rural-farm populations, as in Pacoima, through a type of profile encountered in village populations, as in Bell, to that of Beverly Hills, where the age profile is an extreme form of the urban age structure with a heavy concentration of the population in the productive years, here, between the ages of thirty and fifty-five.

The age profiles shown in figure 32 are extreme forms within the age pattern of Los Angeles itself. In these populations, the proportion of persons twenty to fifty years of age approximates that of the total urban population, but the child population is very small and population in the older ages is disproportionately high.

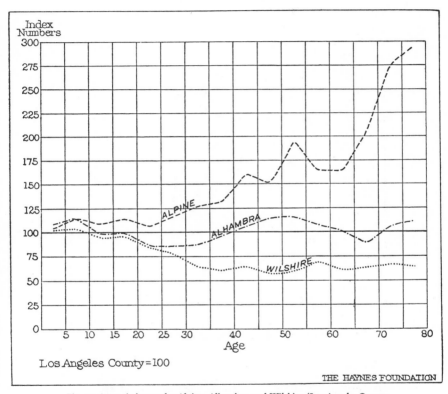

Fig. 33. Sex ratio by age for Alpine, Alhambra, and Wilshire (Los Angeles County census tracts 116, 477, and 101).

There are important differences in the position occupied by populations belonging to these two broad categories. Those populations in which the proportion of people in the working ages is either deficient or in excess of the average are sharply differentiated from one another in the level of occupation and income and in the level of schooling. The populations with characteristic old-age profiles, on the other hand, are found at all levels of occupation, education, and income. The explanation is that the age profiles of populations in the productive years of life are sharply influenced by differences in work situations and by the differential demands and pressures of the urban economic organization. Populations in the older ages are not affected by these differential demands of the economy, but the prior position occupied by the working population carries over into old age, with the result

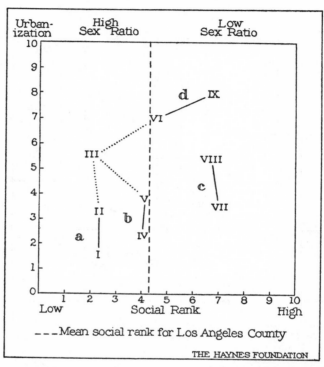

Fig. 34. Relation of age profiles to structure of social areas. Numerals indicate the position of social areas in relation to social rank and urbanization. Letters show the grouping of social areas in four general age types.

that, in the city, populations with old-age profiles are encountered in the very high income, the very low income, and intermediate positions. There is one important difference. In populations in high and intermediate positions, older-age women tend to be dominant. In low levels of occupation and income, populations are heavily weighted with older men. These contrasts in the sex distribution of old-age populations in different social positions are illustrated in figure 33, where index numbers for sex ratios by age are given for three representative populations at three levels of rank.

AGE PROFILES OF POPULATIONS IN LOS ANGELES

As is suggested by the foregoing material on Los Angeles, the age profiles of representative populations fall into several distinct groups. We identify them here as Age Profiles of the General Type A, B, C, or D, and indicate their relation to the structure of social areas in figure 34. Social areas indicated by numerals are shown in positions determined by their median indexes of social rank and urbanization. Letters referring to the four general age types are given opposite the social areas in which the type is characteristic. Type A is characteristic in social areas I and II; type B, in areas IV and V; type C, in areas VII and VIII; and type D, in areas VI and IX. Types A, B, and D are found in area III which, in the diagram, is related to each type by a dotted line.

The population of Pacoima is chosen as being representative of type A, and the population of North Hollywood, of type B. Beverly Hills stands for type C; Wilshire, for type D.

The characteristics of each type of age profile are described in some detail by means of tabular and diagrammatic material on pages 89–121. On each page, representative populations other than the ones mentioned are given separately for each type, with identifying place name, social area, and census-tract designations. When not otherwise indicated, illustrations following are for places in Los Angeles County. Numerical data descriptive of each type include median occupation level[7] of each population selected as representative of the type, median age, sex ratio, median years of schooling, and median rent. On the page given to each type, representative populations from other cities selected on an empirical basis are included, and the characteristics of each are given.

That these age profiles are significant demographic forms asso-

---

[7] The "occupation level" is introduced in this section as one alternative method of measuring the occupational status of populations. It differs from the ratio used as a part of the index of social rank in the following respects.

The ratio used in the index of social rank to measure occupational status is the percentage of employed persons represented by three of the classifications with lowest status: craftsmen, operatives, and laborers. As this percentage increases, there is a reciprocal decrease in the percentage of persons in the remaining higher classifications. However, these remaining classifications vary considerably in status from the professional managerial group to the service group. Two populations (tracts) with equal percentages of employed persons classified as craftsmen, operatives, and laborers, might differ in status as a result of differences in the composition of the rest of the working population.

The occupation level is a figure which represents a grading on a scale which includes all occupations ranked by status as described below. The figure is sensitive to variations in the number of employed persons in any classification, not merely in three of the lowest.

An examination of the relative position of census tracts, when ranked by occupation level as compared with their ranking by the occupation ratio used in the index of social rank, reveals differences

ciated with social position and productive functions in society is shown by the fact that populations with age profiles exactly like those found in Los Angeles are readily identified by using simple empirical procedures in the analysis of the census-tract data for other cities. Tract designations and census characteristics of these populations from other cities are shown following the numerical data for Los Angeles for each of the types.

That the age profiles, which we can thus identify in Los Angeles and other urban areas, are highly stable demographic forms, is suggested by the fact that, in the instances so far examined, changes in numbers do not alter the fundamental features of any of the types. This is shown by a comparison of 1940 and 1946 data for Los Angeles. For each of the types, 1940 and 1946 age profiles have been traced on the same diagram for a number of tracts in Los Angeles, where fairly important population changes occurred between those two dates. In the instances illustrated, population changes range from a decrease of 6 per cent through increases of 60 and 80, up to an increase of 137 per cent. In one instance, nearly 4,000 per cent increase in population has occurred. In all, the alterations of the age profile were not sufficient to change the basic features of the type represented.

---

which appear significant when checked against related figures such as rent. However, the differences are only rarely great enough to change the gross position of the tracts for social rank from low, middle, or high level. Therefore, for the purpose of the classification of tracts by social areas, the occupation ratio first described has been retained. The occupation level may be found useful when a finer classification is desired.

In order to compute the median occupational level for each census tract, a ranking by status was made as follows:

High 8
        Professional workers
    7
        Semiprofessional workers
    6
        Proprietors, managers, and officials
    5
        Clerical, sales, and kindred workers
    4
        Craftsmen, foremen, and kindred workers
    3
        Operatives and kindred workers
    2
        Service workers, except domestic
    1
        Laborers
Low 0

The occupation groups are those used by the Bureau of the Census, with the omission of two groups: "Occupation not reported" and "Domestic service workers." The reason for the omission of the former seems obvious; that for the latter may need some clarification. "Domestic service workers" as a group was omitted inasmuch as its living arrangements are usually atypical: domestics live on the premises of families whose income status is high enough to enable them to command this service, but the domestics obviously do not belong to the same social level. Therefore, to consider them as a part of these areas would distort the facts considerably—as, for example, in Beverly Hills, where domestics comprise the largest group of employed persons.

TABLE 18

AGE PROFILES OF GENERAL TYPE A

Social area	Identifying place name	Census tract	Median occupation level	Median age	Sex ratio	Median years schooling	Median rent
II S	Watts.............	286	2.10	25	99	7.5	16.5
III S	Wholesale..........	116	2.33	29	129	5.9	15.8
II S	Lincoln Heights....	120	2.57	26	104	6.9	18.9
I S	Willowbrook.......	527	2.80	26	105	8.2	18.1
II S	Pacoima..........	4	2.80	25	106	8.3	18.5
II	Torrance..........	289	2.81	29	104	8.8	22.2
	Potrero, San Francisco...........	L-4	2.62	30	101	7.5	26.7
	Highland Park, Seattle..........	S-2	3.03	30	110	8.9	17.8

SOURCE: United States Census, 1940.

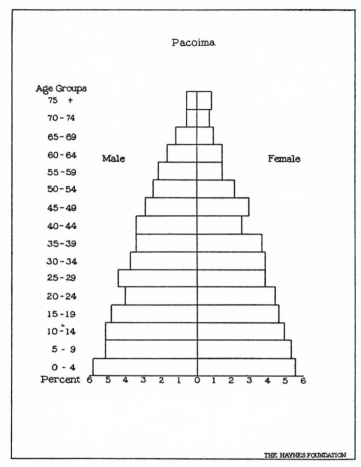

Fig. 35. Age pyramid for Pacoima (census tract 4).

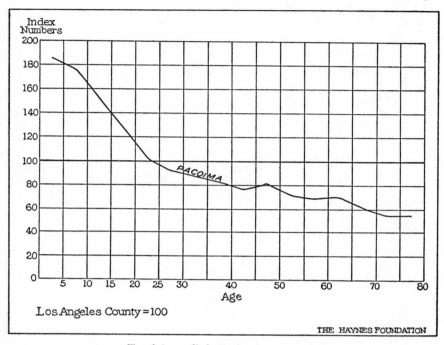

Fig. 36. Age profile for Pacoima (census tract 4).

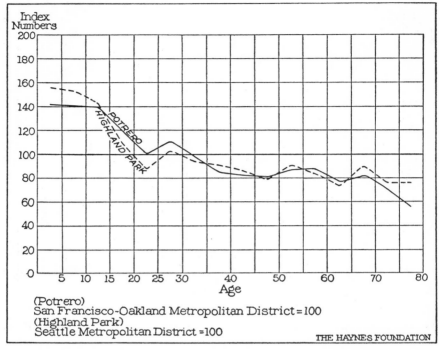

Fig. 37. Age profiles: Potrero, San Francisco (census tract L-4); Highland Park, Seattle (census tract S-2).

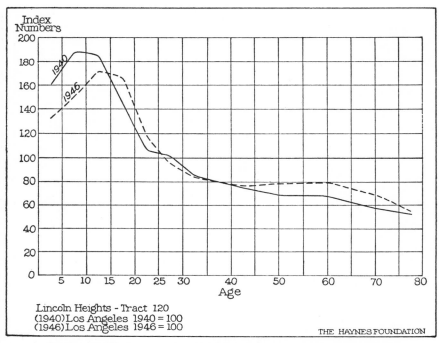

Fig. 38. Age profiles for 1940 and 1946 in Lincoln Heights (census tract 120). Decrease in population, 6.0 per cent.

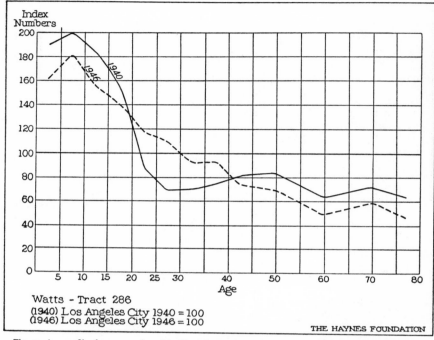

Watts - Tract 286
(1940) Los Angeles City 1940 = 100
(1946) Los Angeles City 1946 = 100

Fig. 39. Age profiles for 1940 and 1946 in Watts (census tract 286). Increase in population, 68.8 per cent.

TABLE 19

AGE PROFILES OF GENERAL TYPE B

Social area	Identifying place name	Census tract	Median occupation level	Median age	Sex ratio	Median years schooling	Median rent
IV	North Long Beach..	330	3.22	31	101	10.5	29.3
V	Lynwood..........	526	3.45	30	101	10.6	28.1
V	Culver City........	368	3.47	31	105	10.7	31.4
V	North Hollywood...	21	4.14	32	101	11.9	39.9
V	Leimert...........	229	4.23	34	89	12.0	39.8
IV S	San Gabriel.......	471	4.32	31	98	11.3	36.8
	Ingleside, San Francisco...........	O-8	3.61	33	102	9.0	33.9

SOURCE: United States Census, 1940.

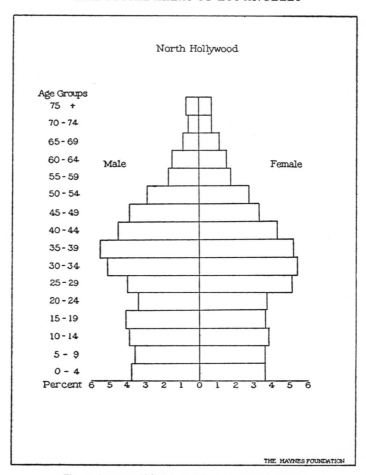

Fig. 40. Age pyramid for North Hollywood (census tract 21).

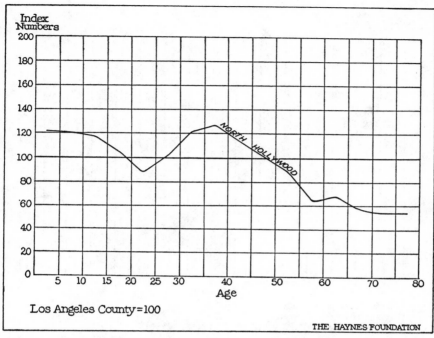

Fig. 41. Age profile for North Hollywood (census tract 21).

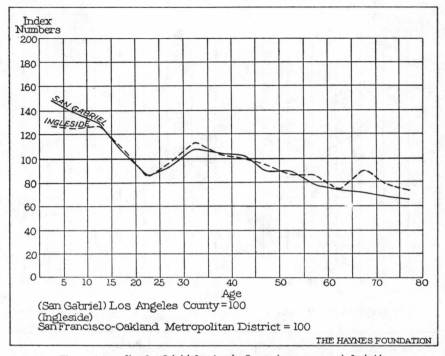

Fig. 42. Age profiles: San Gabriel, Los Angeles County (census tract 471); Ingleside, San Francisco (census tract O-8).

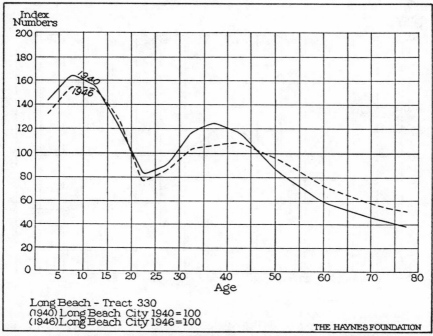

Fig. 43. Age profiles for 1940 and 1946 in Long Beach (census tract 330). Increase in population, 80.2 per cent.

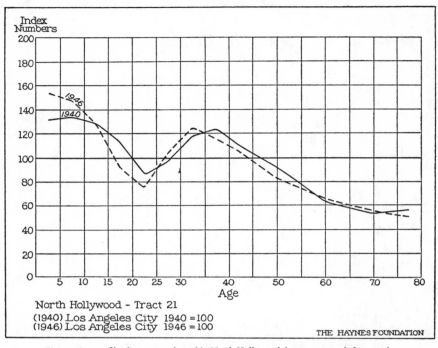

Fig. 44. Age profiles for 1940 and 1946 in North Hollywood (census tract 21). Increase in population, 137.6 per cent.

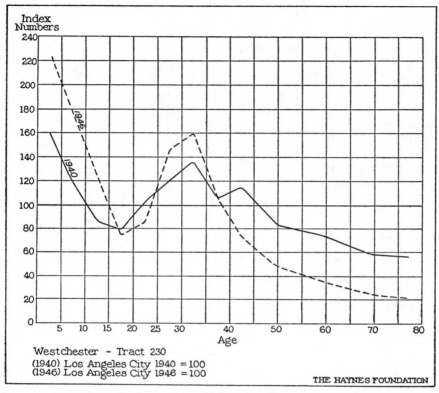

Westchester – Tract 230
(1940) Los Angeles City 1940 = 100
(1946) Los Angeles City 1946 = 100

Fig. 45. Age profiles for 1940 and 1946 in Westchester (census tract 230). Population increased by 14,004 persons (from 353 to 14,357).

TABLE 20

AGE PROFILES OF GENERAL TYPE C

Social area	Identifying place name	Census tract	Median occupation level	Median age	Sex ratio	Median years schooling	Median rent
VII	Glendale—North...	409	4.95	37	90	12.6	53.3
VII	San Marino........	472	5.43	35	79	12.9	92.9
VIII	Beverly Hills.......	381	5.47	38	72	12.5	100+
	St. Francis Wood,	O-6	4.70	38	88	12.2	56.2
	San Francisco....	O-7	5.11	38	87	12.4	81.7
	Winnetka, Illinois...	...	5.13	34	79	13.0	....
	Sea Cliff, San Francisco...........	E-1	5.22	38	76	12.6	86.0
	Bronxville, New York............	...	5.32	36	75	12.7	....
	Shaker Heights, Cleveland........	SH-5	5.36	35	79	12.8	100+

SOURCE: United States Census, 1940.

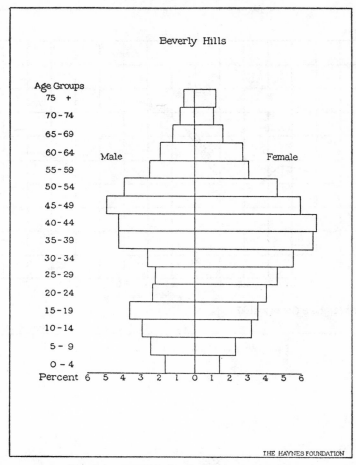

Fig. 46. Age pyramid for Beverly Hills (census tract 381).

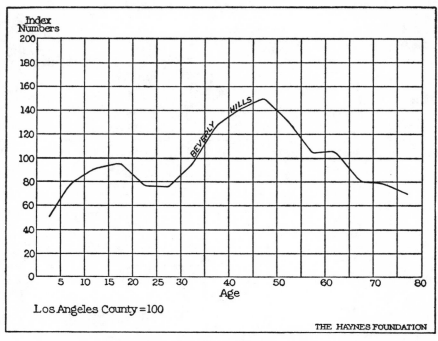

Fig. 47. Age profile for Beverly Hills (census tract 381).

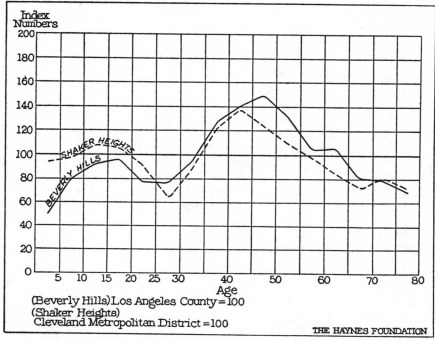

Fig. 48. Age profiles: Shaker Heights, Cleveland (census tract SH-5); Beverly Hills, Los Angeles County (census tract 381).

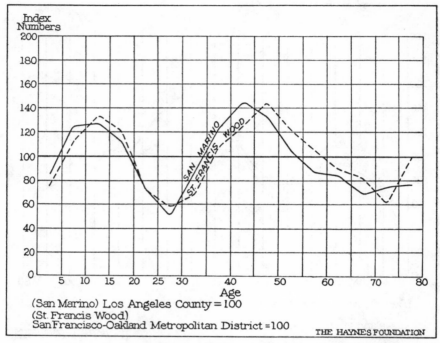

Fig. 49. Age profiles: San Marino, Los Angeles County (census tract 472); St. Francis Wood, San Francisco (census tract O-6).

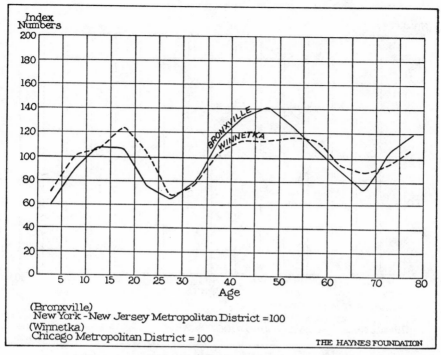

Fig. 50. Age profiles for Bronxville, New York, and Winnetka, Illinois.

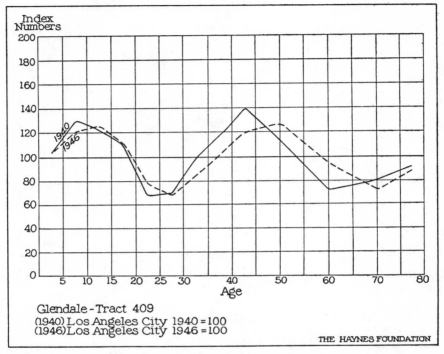

Glendale - Tract 409
(1940) Los Angeles City 1940 = 100
(1946) Los Angeles City 1946 = 100

THE HAYNES FOUNDATION

Fig. 51. Age profiles for 1940 and 1946 in Glendale (census tract 409). Increase in population, 34.8 per cent.

TABLE 21

AGE PROFILES OF GENERAL TYPE D

Social area	Identifying place name	Census tract	Median occupation level	Median age	Sex ratio	Median years schooling	Median rent
		HIGH SOCIAL RANK					
IX	Wilshire...........	109	4.48	44	60	12.3	36.8
IX	Wilshire...........	100	4.63	43	68	12.4	51.1
IX	Pasadena—Central..	428	4.49	49	59	12.3	34.1
	Nob Hill, San Francisco............	A-12	4.52	42	63	12.3	41.1
	Beacon Hill, Boston.	K-2	4.84	41	54	12.5	70.6
		MIDDLE SOCIAL RANK					
VI	Echo Park.........	114	4.06	40	76	10.9	27.6
VI	Westlake..........	110	4.31	44	84	11.9	32.4
		LOW SOCIAL RANK					
III S	Little Tokyo.......	187	2.52	46	403	7.9	12.3
	Howard Street, San Francisco.......	K-3	2.19	46	339	7.5	15.2
	South End, Boston..	L-4	2.34	44	116	8.0	20.2

SOURCE: United States Census, 1940.

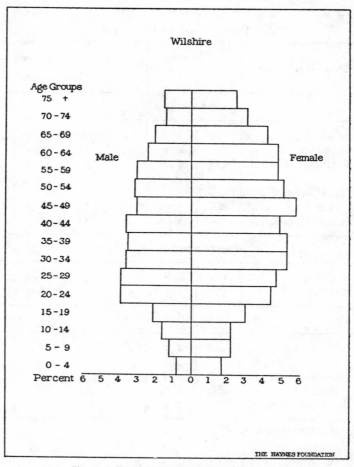

Fig. 52. Age pyramid for Wilshire (census tract 100).

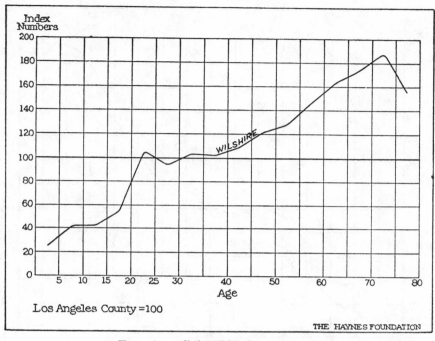

Fig. 53. Age profile for Wilshire (census tract 100).

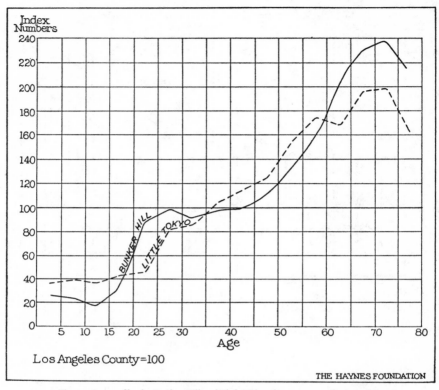

Fig. 54. Age profiles for Bunker Hill and Little Tokyo (census tracts 181 and 187).

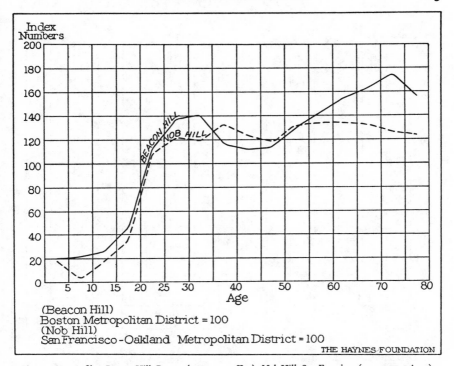

Fig. 55. Age profiles: Beacon Hill, Boston (census tract K-2); Nob Hill, San Francisco (census tract A-12).

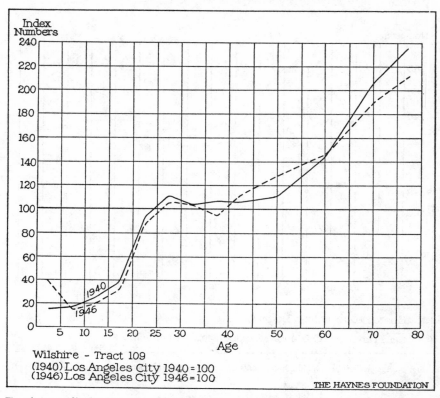

Fig. 56. Age profiles for 1940 and 1946 in Wilshire (census tract 109). Increase in population, 22.2 per cent.

TABLE 22

AGE PROFILES OF GENERAL TYPE B-2

Social area	Identifying place name	Census tract	Median occupation level	Median age	Sex ratio	Median years schooling	Median rent
IV S	Duarte...........	446	2.87	32	86	10.0	17.3
III S	Lincoln Heights....	72	2.92	31	92	8.4	23.8
IV S	Irwindale.........	447	2.94	31	103	8.7	7.8
V S	Monrovia.........	445	3.17	32	97	8.8	21.8
IV S	Downey..........	541	3.38	37	125	10.2	24.4
V	Sunland..........	7	3.53	35	98	10.0	23.3
V	Sierra Madre.......	443	4.36	39	87	12.0	27.6
	Strongsville, Cleveland...........	CC-13	3.68	32	104	8.9	26.4

SOURCE: United States Census, 1940.

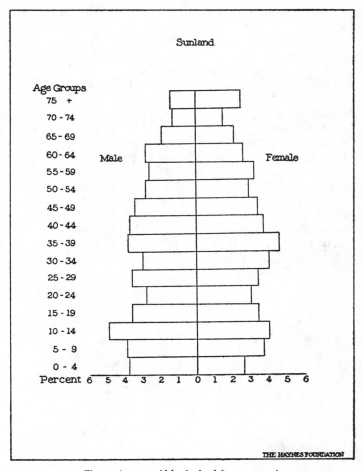

Fig. 57. Age pyramid for Sunland (census tract 7).

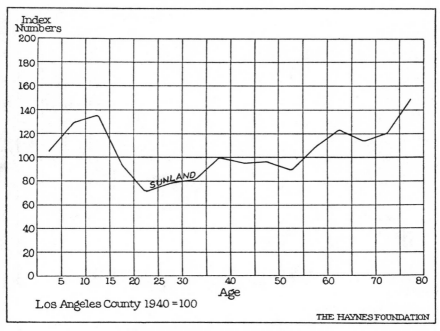

Fig. 58. Age profile for Sunland (census tract 7).

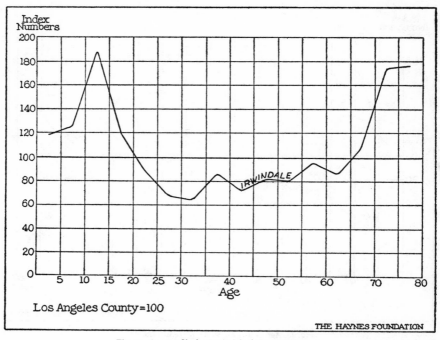

Fig. 59. Age profile for Irwindale (census tract 447).

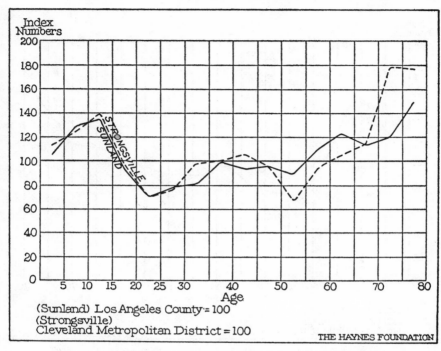

Fig. 60. Age profiles: Sunland, Los Angeles County (census tract 7); Strongsville, Cleveland (census tract CC-13).

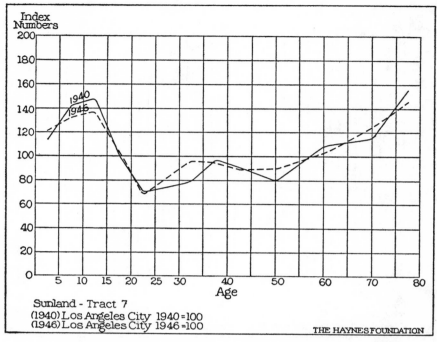

Fig. 61. Age profiles for 1940 and 1946 in Sunland (census tract 7). Increase in population, 60.6 per cent.

TABLE 23

SUMMARY OF CHARACTERISTICS BY AGE TYPE

Type	Representative population	Census tract	Median occupation level	Median age	Sex ratio	Median years schooling	Median rent
A	Pacoima............	4	2.80	25	106	8.3	18.5
B	North Hollywood...	21	4.14	32	101	11.9	39.9
C	Beverly Hills.......	381	5.47	38	72	12.5	100+
D	Wilshire...........	100	4.63	43	68	12.4	51.1
B-2	Sunland...........	7	3.53	35	98	10.0	23.3

SOURCE: United States Census, 1940.

APPENDIXES

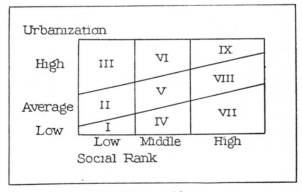

Fig. 62. Key to social areas.

[124]

APPENDIX A

Census tract	Identifying place name	Social rank	Urbani-zation	Segrega-tion	Social area
1	Sylmar........................	36	38	28	V S
2	Chatsworth....................	31	24	15	V S
3	Granada Hills..................	36	32	9	V
4	Pacoima.......................	20	17	35	II S
5	Roscoe........................	24	15	3	I
6	Sunland.......................	38	33	11	V
7	Sunland.......................	36	27	5	V
8	Northridge....................	27	27	23	II S
9	Sepulveda.....................	28	23	9	II
10	Roscoe........................	28	21	11	II
11	Verdugo Hills..................	39	25	2	IV
12	Tujunga.......................	40	28	3	V
13	Canoga Park—Environs..........	35	25	11	V
14	Canoga Park...................	23	18	41	I S
15	Canoga Park—Environs..........	33	28	7	V
16	Reseda........................	30	18	4	IV
17	Van Nuys......................	40	29	11	V
18	Van Nuys......................	44	29	2	V
19	Roscoe........................	30	22	8	V
20	North Hollywood...............	54	33	2	V
21	North Hollywood...............	50	32	2	V
22	North Hollywood...............	33	29	13	V
23	North Hollywood...............	56	41	1	V
24	North Hollywood...............	63	36	3	VIII
25	Studio City....................	62	39	3	VIII
26	Woodland Hills.................	39	28	11	V
27	Tarzana.......................	41	37	3	V
28	Encino........................	53	39	5	V
29	Sherman Oaks..................	55	33	2	V
30	Hollywood Hills................	77	64	5	VIII
31	Griffith Park..................	53	40	9	V
32	Silver Lake....................	65	49	7	VIII
33	Eagle Rock—Hill Drive..........	62	37	1	VIII
34	Eagle Rock....................	52	40	1	V
35	Eagle Rock....................	46	37	1	V
36	Highland Park.................	42	33	3	V
37	Mount Washington.............	33	30	6	V
38	Mount Washington.............	32	40	7	V
39	Mount Washington.............	31	36	9	V

APPENDIX A—*Continued*

Census tract	Identifying place name	Social rank	Urbani-zation	Segrega-tion	Social area
40	Highland Park..................	43	46	2	V
41	Highland Park..................	41	36	2	V
42	Highland Park..................	40	36	3	V
43	Highland Park..................	44	46	2	V
44	Highland Park..................	43	37	1	V
45	Highland Park..................	42	44	2	V
46	Highland Park..................	44	58	2	V
47	Highland Park..................	39	38	2	V
48	Pacific Palisades, Brentwood, Bel-Air	82	46	7	VIII
49	Beverly Crest...................	68	42	5	VIII
50	Beverly Crest...................	86	45	5	VII
51	West Hollywood................	77	48	6	VIII
52	Hollywood Hills................	72	63	6	VIII
53	Hollywood—Central.............	67	80	4	IX
54	Hollywood—Central.............	57	75	8	VI
55	Hollywood—Central.............	69	81	4	IX
56	Hollywood—Central.............	61	74	7	IX
57	West Hollywood................	66	62	4	VIII
58	Hollywood Hills................	67	69	5	VIII
59	Silver Lake.....................	48	59	8	V
60	Atwater........................	43	35	5	V
61	Atwater........................	38	35	3	V
62	Silver Lake.....................	56	61	7	V
63	Silver Lake.....................	48	53	6	V
64	Elysian Park....................	44	51	5	V
65	Lincoln Heights.................	32	29	9	V
66	Elysian Park....................	42	56	7	V
67	Chavez Ravine..................	13	29	70	II S
68	Lincoln Heights.................	25	40	10	II
69	Lincoln Heights.................	30	45	30	V S
70	Lincoln Heights.................	35	44	6	V
71	Lincoln Heights.................	32	41	20	V S
72	Lincoln Heights.................	25	53	26	III S
73	Lincoln Heights.................	26	41	:7	II S
74	Bairdstown, El Sereno............	40	35	13	V
75	Bairdstown, El Sereno............	40	30	3	V
76	West Hollywood................	62	55	5	VIII
77	West Hollywood................	59	57	5	V
78	Hollywood—S.W................	57	61	4	V
79	West Wilshire..................	69	66	6	VIII
80	West Wilshire..................	71	80	8	IX
81	Beverly-Fairfax................	54	71	17	VI S

APPENDIX A—*Continued*

Census tract	Identifying place name	Social rank	Urbani-zation	Segrega-tion	Social area
82	West Wilshire	75	68	8	VIII
83	Hollywood—S.W.	57	77	9	VI
84	Hollywood—S.W.	52	73	7	VI
85	Hollywood—S.E.	53	70	6	VI
86	Hollywood—S.E.	60	82	5	IX
87	Silver Lake	48	69	16	VI S
88	Hollywood—S.W.	41	59	6	VI
89	Hollywood—S.W.	53	75	5	VI
90	Hollywood—S.E.	55	66	5	VI
91	Hollywood—S.E.	62	65	4	VIII
92	Silver Lake	56	72	4	VI
93	Wilshire	78	62	4	VIII
94	Hollywood—S.W.	62	67	4	VIII
95	Hollywood—S.E.	61	68	4	IX
96	Hollywood—S.E.	63	83	3	IX
97	Beverly-Melrose, Vermont-Hoover	40	55	40	V S
98	Wilshire	80	51	7	VIII
99	Wilshire	74	73	5	VIII
100	Wilshire	71	78	3	IX
101	Wilshire	71	94	5	IX
102	Wilshire	66	80	4	IX
103	Silver Lake	53	77	7	VI
104	Silver Lake	52	67	5	VI
105	Echo Park	44	65	12	VI
106	Westlake	57	71	22	VI S
107	Westlake	53	75	16	VI S
108	Westlake	51	85	10	VI
109	Wilshire	70	89	4	IX
110	Westlake	58	91	4	VI
111	Westlake	57	96	2	VI
112	Westlake	53	93	4	VI
113	Temple Street	34	57	35	VI S
114	Echo Park	47	66	10	VI
115	Temple Street	33	55	42	V S
116	Wholesale	17	53	98	III S
117	Downtown	40	69	66	VI S
118	Wholesale	10	40	90	II S
119	Wholesale	8	27	83	II S
120	Lincoln Heights	9	38	61	II S
121	Boyle Heights	7	38	85	II S
122	Boyle Heights	15	46	64	II S
123	Boyle Heights	35	51	32	V S

APPENDIX A—*Continued*

Census tract	Identifying place name	Social rank	Urbani-zation	Segrega-tion	Social area
124	Boyle Heights	20	35	46	II S
125	Boyle Heights	19	47	68	II S
126	Boyle Heights	25	51	36	II S
127	Boyle Heights	25	49	46	II S
128	Boyle Heights	32	62	42	VI S
129	Boyle Heights	30	42	62	V S
130	Boyle Heights	22	35	67	II S
131	Boyle Heights	23	49	48	II S
132	Boyle Heights	20	36	47	II S
133	Boyle Heights	23	34	38	II S
134	Boyle Heights	25	36	14	II S
135	Boyle Heights	30	46	41	V S
136	Bairdstown, El Sereno	36	27	5	V
137	Bairdstown, El Sereno	41	30	2	V
138	Westwood	83	54	4	VIII
139	Westwood	65	42	1	VIII
140	Westgate	60	39	4	VIII
141	West Los Angeles	38	43	6	V
142	West Los Angeles	33	38	14	V S
143	Sawtelle	25	35	30	II S
144	Mar Vista	42	29	3	V
145	Cheviot Hills	68	43	3	VIII
146	Palms	50	37	2	V
147	Palms	39	44	2	V
148	Wilshire-Pico	70	63	6	VIII
149	Wilshire-Pico	69	68	5	VIII
150	Wilshire-Pico	71	65	5	VIII
151	Wilshire-Pico	66	59	7	VIII
152	Wilshire-Pico	66	56	5	VIII
153	Wilshire-Pico	60	57	4	VIII
154	Wilshire-Pico	61	67	6	VIII
155	Wilshire-Pico	62	49	5	VIII
156	West Adams	51	53	4	V
157	West Adams	55	54	4	V
158	West Adams	44	39	6	V
159	West Adams	46	55	7	V
160	Wilshire	73	57	5	VIII
161	Wilshire	63	73	4	IX
162	Pico-Vermont	56	72	3	VI
163	Wilshire	68	64	7	VIII
164	Wilshire	76	84	5	IX
165	Wilshire	68	90	5	IX

APPENDIX A—*Continued*

Census tract	Identifying place name	Social rank	Urbani- zation	Segrega- tion	Social area
166	Pico-Vermont	51	70	24	VI S
167	Pico-Vermont	42	62	26	VI S
168	Pico-Vermont	59	75	4	VI
169	Pico-Vermont	46	65	6	VI
170	Pico-Vermont	53	92	3	VI
171	Pico-Vermont	43	69	8	VI
172	Westlake	54	87	5	VI
173	Downtown	46	90	4	VI
174	Westlake	51	85	3	VI
175	Downtown	39	78	3	VI
176	Westlake	49	85	5	VI
177	Downtown	36	74	6	VI
178	Figueroa-Adams	46	84	5	VI
179	Figueroa-Adams	37	75	9	VI
180	Bunker Hill	33	70	26	VI S
181	Bunker Hill	41	82	9	VI
182	Downtown	48	88	5	VI
183	Downtown	53	84	4	VI
184	Downtown	39	93	9	VI
185	Downtown	40	88	17	VI S
186	Little Tokyo	32	87	36	VI S
187	Little Tokyo	25	69	28	III S
188	Little Tokyo	20	63	49	III S
189	Little Tokyo	25	54	82	III S
190	Venice	38	27	2	V
191	Venice	32	32	9	V
192	Venice	36	54	12	V
193	Venice	36	34	3	V
194	Venice	45	42	4	V
195	Playa Del Rey	68	39	3	VIII
196	Del Rey	30	23	14	V S
197	West Adams	38	35	5	V
198	West Adams	38	33	7	V
199	West Adams	46	52	15	V S
200	West Adams	45	56	12	V
201	West Adams	59	66	6	V
202	West Adams	36	40	10	V
203	Berkeley Square	59	67	10	VI
204	West Jefferson	49	58	67	V S
205	West Jefferson	40	43	43	V S
206	South Vermont	47	54	5	V
207	Leimert	62	54	4	VIII

APPENDIX A—*Continued*

Census tract	Identifying place name	Social rank	Urbani- zation	Segrega- tion	Social area
208	West Adams Heights............	55	67	6	VI
209	West Jefferson..................	43	67	20	VI S
210	West Jefferson..................	38	67	13	VI
211	West Jefferson..................	50	68	8	VI
212	West Jefferson..................	47	45	6	V
213	West Jefferson..................	45	65	12	VI
214	West Jefferson..................	43	52	91	V S
215	West Jefferson..................	40	56	46	V S
216	West Jefferson..................	48	69	11	VI
217	South Vermont..................	48	57	3	V
218	Exposition Park.................	50	67	4	VI
219	Figueroa-Adams.................	46	73	14	VI S
220	Figueroa-Adams.................	35	89	13	VI
221	Figueroa-Adams.................	33	71	19	VI S
222	Figueroa-Adams.................	36	69	18	VI S
223	Central Avenue..................	20	58	77	III S
224	Central Avenue..................	25	47	92	II S
225	Central Avenue..................	30	56	79	VI S
226	Central Avenue..................	32	57	96	VI S
227	Central Avenue..................	31	52	85	V S
228	Leimert........................	50	46	2	V
229	Leimert........................	51	39	2	V
230	Westchester....................	50	22	5	IV
231	Leimert........................	52	49	2	V
232	Leimert........................	43	37	2	V
233	Leimert........................	45	33	2	V
234	South Vermont..................	50	47	3	V
235	Exposition Park.................	49	63	4	VI
236	Exposition Park.................	47	72	6	VI
237	South Vermont..................	47	55	2	V
238	South Vermont..................	44	54	4	V
239	Exposition Park.................	41	62	7	VI
240	South Vermont..................	42	52	2	V
241	South Vermont..................	41	50	5	V
242	South Vermont..................	37	49	6	V
243	Exposition Park.................	43	75	8	VI
244	Exposition Park.................	38	66	10	VI
245	Exposition Park.................	36	61	9	VI
246	Exposition Park.................	32	55	8	VI
247	Central Avenue..................	26	51	37	II S
248	Central Avenue..................	37	57	77	V S
249	Central Avenue..................	37	58	69	VI S

APPENDIX A—*Continued*

Census tract	Identifying place name	Social rank	Urbani-zation	Segrega-tion	Social area
250	Central Avenue..................	37	55	52	V S
251	Central Avenue..................	33	52	51	V S
252	Central Avenue..................	43	57	96	V S
253	Central Avenue..................	22	36	83	II S
254	Central Avenue..................	38	57	94	V S
255	Central Avenue..................	29	36	90	II S
256	Central Avenue..................	31	42	85	V S
257	South Vermont..................	36	36	4	V
258	South Vermont..................	35	47	4	V
259	South Vermont..................	48	40	2	V
260	South Vermont..................	39	42	3	V
261	South Vermont..................	36	48	4	V
262	South Vermont..................	50	37	2	V
263	South Vermont..................	43	38	3	V
264	South Vermont..................	37	48	3	V
265	South Vermont..................	51	34	2	V
266	South Vermont..................	48	44	2	V
267	South Vermont..................	38	48	3	V
268	Green Meadows..................	28	45	6	II
269	Green Meadows..................	23	36	6	II
270	Green Meadows..................	30	44	5	V
271	Green Meadows..................	26	37	4	II
272	Green Meadows..................	28	42	6	II
273	Green Meadows..................	28	39	7	II
274	Green Meadows..................	30	39	4	V
275	Green Meadows..................	28	32	7	II
276	South Vermont..................	48	31	2	V
277	Green Meadows..................	33	32	3	V
278	Green Meadows..................	42	36	2	V
279	Green Meadows..................	31	34	6	V
280	Green Meadows..................	26	27	6	II
281	Green Meadows..................	28	32	4	II
282	Green Meadows..................	26	31	3	II
283	Green Meadows..................	20	21	2	II
284	Green Meadows..................	27	26	4	II
285	Watts..........................	20	23	34	II S
286	Watts..........................	20	22	90	II S
287	Watts..........................	11	14	84	II S
288	Gardena.......................	34	27	16	V S
289	Torrance......................	22	25	8	II
290	Wilmington....................	30	43	15	V S
291	Wilmington....................	34	38	2	V

APPENDIX A—*Continued*

Census tract	Identifying place name	Social rank	Urbani-zation	Segrega-tion	Social area
292	Wilmington.....................	16	30	39	II S
293	Wilmington.....................	23	50	34	II S
294	Terminal Island.................	10	65	75	III S
295	San Pedro—Industrial...........	29	30	22	II S
296	San Pedro—Industrial...........	17	42	31	II S
297	San Pedro—Industrial...........	25	38	18	II S
298	San Pedro—Commercial..........	40	43	5	V
299	San Pedro—Industrial...........	29	48	16	II S
300	San Pedro—Commercial..........	36	31	4	V
301	San Pedro—Residential...........	54	38	4	V
303	Long Beach—Commercial and Residential......................	30	45	11	V
304	Long Beach—Central............,....	45	67	7	VI
305	Long Beach—Central............	46	64	3	VI
306	Long Beach—Central............	48	67	4	VI
307	Long Beach—Central............	45	59	2	V
308	Long Beach—Central............	46	63	1	VI
309	Long Beach—Central............	47	68	2	VI
310	Long Beach—Central............	49	78	1	VI
311	Long Beach—Central............	56	75	2	VI
312	Long Beach—Belmont Heights....	63	68	1	VIII
313	Long Beach—Commercial and Residential...................	49	59	1	V
314	Long Beach—Commercial and Residential...................	42	48	3	V
315	Long Beach—Commercial and Residential...................	47	49	2	V
316	Long Beach—Commercial and Residential...................	52	49	1	V
317	Long Beach—Belmont Heights....	64	52	1	VIII
318	Long Beach—Belmont Heights....	65	55	1	VIII
319	Long Beach—Belmont Heights....	65	45	2	VIII
320	Long Beach—Commercial and Residential...................	55	46	0	V
321	Long Beach—Commercial and Residential...................	54	41	3	V
322	Long Beach—Commercial and Residential...................	39	31	9	V
323	Long Beach—Commercial and Residential...................	33	38	2	V
324	Long Beach—Commercial and Residential...................	37	44	2	V

APPENDIX A—*Continued*

Census tract	Identifying place name	Social rank	Urbanization	Segregation	Social area
325	Long Beach—Commercial and Residential.................	29	33	9	II
326	Long Beach—Commercial and Residential.................	40	42	3	V
327	Long Beach—Commercial and Residential.................	48	38	5	V
328	Long Beach–California Heights–Bixby Knolls.................	59	34	1	IV
329	North Long Beach...............	38	29	2	V
330	North Long Beach...............	34	22	2	IV
331	San Pedro—Industrial............	38	31	20	V S
332-A	Lakewood Village, Mayfair........	65	30	7	VII
332-C	Long Beach–California Heights–Bixby Knolls.................	70	30	1	VII
332-D	Long Beach[a].....................	48	10	0	IV
333	Long Beach—East...............	24	9	41	I S
334	Signal Hill......................	34	37	2	V
335	Dominguez.....................	28	23	39	II S
336-A	Torrance.......................	34	23	5	V
336-B	Torrance.......................	18	27	9	II
337-A	Rolling Hills...................	50	34	27	V S
337-B	Palos Verdes Estates............	86	36	20	VII S
338	Torrance.......................	23	31	43	II S
339	Torrance.......................	34	33	11	V
340-A	Gardena.......................	23	34	50	II S
340-B	Gardena.......................	32	28	22	V S
340-C	Gardena.......................	20	3	10	I
341-A	Gardena.......................	33	28	20	V S
341-B	Gardena.......................	30	27	16	V S
342-A	Gardena.......................	42	31	5	V
342-B	South Vermont..................	49	31	0	V
343	Gardena.......................	42	35	2	V
345	Inglewood—Hollywood Park......	56	34	5	V
346	Inglewood—West................	42	39	1	V
347	Inglewood—West................	38	26	1	V
348	Inglewood—West................	37	29	4	V
349	Inglewood[a].....................	23	38	0	II
350-A	Hawthorne.....................	36	23	2	IV
350-B	Inglewood—West................	31	28	1	V
351-A	Hawthorne.....................	38	24	3	IV
352	Hawthorne.....................	27	25	4	II

[a] Tract not included in 185 named places.

APPENDIX A—*Continued*

Census tract	Identifying place name	Social rank	Urbanization	Segregation	Social area
353	Hawthorne	33	18	17	IV S
354-A	Hawthorne	23	9	1	I
354-B	Hawthorne	17	18	0	II
354-C	Hawthorne	13	2	71	I S
355	Torrance	25	18	31	I S
356	Redondo Beach*	69	35	17	VII S
357	Redondo Beach	39	38	5	V
358	Hawthorne	19	13	12	I
359	Hermosa Beach	45	40	6	V
360	Manhattan Beach	53	34	2	V
361	El Porto Beach*	61	54	1	VIII
362	El Segundo	34	25	1	V
363	Del Rey	21	50	83	III S
364	Del Rey	13	23	100	II S
365	View Park, Baldwin Hills	84	37	3	VII
367	Palms	46	41	2	V
368	Culver City	39	40	5	V
372	Santa Monica—Ocean Park	37	51	7	V
373	Santa Monica—South	40	52	14	V S
374	Santa Monica—South	39	34	21	V S
375	Santa Monica—South	38	55	11	V
376	Santa Monica—Central	57	71	1	VI
377	Santa Monica—South	34	41	18	V S
378	Santa Monica—North	51	50	2	V
379	Santa Monica—North	67	48	2	VIII
380	Sawtelle–Government Reservation	45	79	6	VI
381	Beverly Hills	91	53	4	VIII
382	Beverly Hills	76	64	3	VIII
383	Beverly Hills	70	67	3	VIII
385	West Hollywood	68	60	3	VIII
386	West Hollywood	51	48	6	V
387	West Hollywood	74	64	6	VIII
390	Burbank	50	33	2	V
391	Burbank	39	28	5	V
392	Burbank	44	24	3	IV
393	Burbank	54	33	1	V
394	Burbank	38	49	10	V
395	Glendale—South	71	26	0	VII
397	Glendale—South	54	31	1	IV
398-A	Glendale—South	41	33	3	V
399	Glendale—North	64	40	1	VIII

* Tract not included in 185 named places.

APPENDIX A—*Continued*

Census tract	Identifying place name	Social rank	Urbani- zation	Segrega- tion	Social area
400	Glendale—South................	51	37	1	V
401	Glendale—South................	51	56	2	V
402	Glendale—South................	46	55	3	V
403	Glendale—South................	43	55	12	V
404	Glendale—South................	54	48	2	V
405	Glendale—South................	52	51	2	V
406	Glendale—Central..............	50	69	2	VI
407	Glendale—South................	50	61	2	V
408	Glendale—North...............	67	38	1	VIII
409	Glendale—North...............	69	35	1	VII
410	Glendale—North...............	60	50	1	VIII
411	Glendale—North...............	63	48	1	VIII
412	Pasadena—Commercial and Resi- dential......................	53	46	1	V
413	Pasadena—Commercial and Resi- dential......................	47	41	2	V
414	Pasadena—Lincoln Avenue.......	36	33	9	V
415	Pasadena—Linda Vista..........	74	46	3	VIII
416	Pasadena—Linda Vista..........	71	48	11	VIII
417	Pasadena—Lincoln Avenue.......	35	42	64	V S
418	Pasadena—Commercial and Resi- dential......................	47	43	6	V
419	Pasadena—Commercial and Resi- dential......................	50	41	2	V
420	Pasadena—East Orange Grove....	62	34	1	VII
421	Pasadena—East Colorado........	41	28	20	V S
422-A	Pasadena—Commercial and Resi- dential......................	46	34	2	V
422-B	Pasadena—Commercial and Resi- dential......................	49	42	1	V
423	Pasadena—Commercial and Resi- dential......................	47	50	4	V
424	Pasadena—Central..............	52	70	2	VI
425	Pasadena—Lincoln Avenue.......	32	50	13	V
426	Pasadena—Annandale...........	73	40	3	VII
427	Pasadena—Lincoln Avenue.......	48	50	42	V S
428	Pasadena—Central..............	61	73	4	IX
429	Pasadena—Oak Knoll............	63	56	3	VIII
430	Pasadena—Commercial and Resi- dential......................	59	43	2	V
431	Pasadena—Commercial and Resi- dential......................	50	35	2	V

APPENDIX A—*Continued*

Census tract	Identifying place name	Social rank	Urbanization	Segregation	Social area
432	Pasadena—Oak Knoll............	69	48	13	VIII
433	Pasadena—Oak Knoll............	70	51	9	VIII
434-A	Altadena......................	59	30	1	IV
435	Altadena......................	70	37	2	VII
436	Altadena......................	89	38	2	VII
437	Altadena......................	70	33	1	VII
438-A	Altadena......................	64	34	7	VII
438-B	Santa Anita Oaks..............	100	45	0	VII
439	San Marino....................	84	36	2	VII
440	Lamanda Park.................	56	31	2	IV
441	Temple City...................	65	28	2	VII
442	Arcadia.......................	52	31	7	V
443	Sierra Madre..................	53	33	6	V
444	Monrovia—North..............	51	38	1	V
445	Monrovia—South..............	30	30	29	V S
446	Duarte........................	57	33	35	IV S
447	Irwindale.....................	41	25	44	IV S
448	Azusa.........................	22	22	60	II S
449	Glendora Suburbs[a]	61	38	4	VIII
450	Glendora......................	29	38	15	II S
451	Claremont.....................	61	41	8	VIII
452	Claremont.....................	70	37	12	VII
453	Claremont.....................	59	43	11	V
454	Pomona—North and Southeast...	51	43	1	V
455	Pomona—North and Southeast....	31	36	3	V
456	Pomona—Southwest............	25	32	29	II S
457	Pomona—North and Southeast....	44	41	12	V
458	La Verne......................	22	28	46	II S
459	San Dimas....................	39	32	20	V S
460	Covina........................	56	36	8	V
461	Covina........................	40	47	0	V
462-A	Covina Suburbs[a]	78	40	8	VII
462-B	West Covina—East	68	35	1	VII
463	West Covina—West............	52	35	18	V S
464	Baldwin Park..................	40	22	6	IV
465	Rosemead.....................	44	23	11	IV
466	El Monte......................	35	31	27	V S
467	Garvey........................	32	19	14	IV
468	Garvey........................	37	20	3	IV
469	Wilmar.......................	39	23	2	IV
470	Temple City...................	57	27	3	IV

[a] Tract not included in 185 named places.

APPENDIX A—*Continued*

Census tract	Identifying place name	Social rank	Urbani-zation	Segrega-tion	Social area
471	San Gabriel....................	47	27	24	IV S
472	San Marino....................	83	38	3	VII
473	South Pasadena................	61	49	4	VIII
474	South Pasadena................	58	48	3	V
475	South Pasadena................	66	50	2	VIII
476	Alhambra.....................	55	46	2	V
477	Alhambra.....................	51	37	4	V
478	Alhambra.....................	43	38	4	V
479	Alhambra.....................	50	46	3	V
480	Alhambra.....................	52	36	2	V
481	Monterey Park.................	40	31	2	V
482	Monterey Park.................	34	29	3	V
483	Monterey Park.................	35	31	7	V
484	City Terrace..................	23	37	45	II S
485	Belvedere.....................	17	30	66	II S
486	Belvedere.....................	15	35	68	II S
487	Belvedere Gardens.............	21	29	34	II S
488	Belvedere Gardens.............	25	31	12	II
489	Belvedere Gardens.............	23	30	15	II S
490	Belvedere.....................	3	18	87	II S
491	Belvedere.....................	3	14	79	II S
492	Belvedere Gardens—East........	31	34	5	V
493	Belvedere Gardens—East........	40	40	5	V
494	Belvedere Gardens—East........	53	39	4	V
495	Belvedere Gardens—East........	53	40	2	V
496	Montebello—North.............	47	37	4	V
497	Montebello—South.............	32	32	17	V S
498	Bandini......................	20	14	32	I S
499	Vernon.......................	20	20	34	II S
501	Vernon.......................	11	26	78	II S
502	Vernon[a].....................	14	42	80	II S
503	Maywood......................	27	44	2	II
504	Maywood......................	32	35	1	V
505	Bell.........................	33	34	2	V
506	Bell Gardens.................	23	22	3	II
507	Bell.........................	33	31	1	V
508	Huntington Park..............	41	33	3	V
509	Huntington Park..............	48	57	2	V
510	Huntington Park..............	30	50	7	V
511	Huntington Park..............	41	59	2	VI
512	Firestone Park...............	18	28	8	II

[a] Tract not included in 185 named places.

APPENDIX A—*Continued*

Census tract	Identifying place name	Social rank	Urbani-zation	Segrega-tion	Social area
513	Firestone Park..................	26	32	16	II S
514	Firestone Park..................	31	41	4	V
515	Firestone Park..................	23	34	5	II
516	Firestone Park..................	32	30	6	V
517 .	Watts........................	30	31	37	V S
518	Firestone Park..................	22	23	18	II S
519	Walnut Park..................	64	42	1	VIII
520	Walnut Park..................	67	35	1	VII
521	South Gate....................	43	35	1	V
522	South Gate....................	31	31	1	V
523	South Gate....................	29	24	3	II
524	South Gate....................	27	33	8	II
526	Lynwood......................	36	29	2	V
527	Willowbrook..................	22	16	33	I S
528	Willowbrook..................	38	28	33	V S
529	Willowbrook..................	29	18	31	I S
530	Compton......................	32	33	8	V
531	Compton......................	43	32	2	V
532	Compton......................	36	23	0	IV
534	Compton......................	40	20	2	IV
535	Lynwood Gardens..............	31	12	3	IV
536	Hynes, Clearwater..............	26	16	12	I
537	Bellflower....................	40	27	4	V
538	Artesia......................	25	16	19	I S
539	Norwalk......................	15	21	27	II S
540	Norwalk......................	36	25	27	V S
541	Downey......................	57	26	16	IV S
542	Pico, Rivera..................	38	21	26	IV S
543	Los Nietos....................	35	22	45	IV S
544	Whittier......................	40	29	9	V
545	Whittier......................	52	48	1	V
546	Whittier......................	39	37	1	V
547	Santa Fe Springs..............	47	27	13	IV
548	Puente......................	34	22	29	IV S
549	Walnut, Spadra..............	29	34	12	II
550	Padua Hills[a]..................	32	28	9	V
551	Mount Wilson[a]..............	42	30	10	V
552	Angeles Crest[a]..............	72	42	2	VIII
553	Flintridge....................	83	35	6	VII
554-A	Montrose......................	62	31	3	VII
555	Tujunga......................	42	30	4	V

[a] Tract not included in 185 named places.

APPENDIX A—*Continued*

Census tract	Identifying place name	Social rank	Urbani- zation	Segrega- tion	Social area
556	San Fernando....................	30	34	50	V S
557	El Merrie Del[a]..................	58	41	5	V
558	Acton[a].........................	36	16	16	IV S
559	Little Rock[a]....................	38	12	1	IV
560	Redman[a].......................	39	14	6	IV
561	Lancaster[a]......................	47	27	6	IV
562	Palmdale[a]......................	41	26	8	V
563-A	Fairmont[a]......................	37	17	6	IV
563-B	Gorman[a].......................	45	36	0	V
564	Saugus[a]........................	35	18	15	IV S
565	Calabasas.......................	51	25	4	IV
566	Malibu La Costa.................	70	43	6	VIII
567	Avalon..........................	64	51	19	VIII S
568	San Clemente[a]..................	62	31	11	VII

CENSUS TRACTS WITH A POPULATION OF LESS THAN 50 FOR WHICH
NO INDEXES WERE CALCULATED

302 (ships at sea)	369	389	500
332-B	370	396	525
344	371	398-B	533
351-B	384	434-B	554-B
366	388	438-C	554-C

[a] Tract not included in 185 named places.

APPENDIX B

Census Tracts by Social Areas, with Indexes of Social Rank,
Urbanization, and Segregation

AREA I

Low social rank. Low index of urbanization

Low Index of Segregation

Census tract	Social rank	Urbani- zation	Segrega- tion	Census tract	Social rank	Urbani- zation	Segrega- tion
5	24	15	3	358	19	13	12
340-C	20	3	10	536	26	16	12
354-A	23	9	1				

High Index of Segregation

Census tract	Social rank	Urbani- zation	Segrega- tion	Census tract	Social rank	Urbani- zation	Segrega- tion
14	23	18	41	498	20	14	32
333	24	9	41	527	22	16	33
354-C	13	2	71	529	29	18	31
355	25	18	31	538	25	16	19

AREA II

Low social rank. Average index of urbanization

Low Index of Segregation

Census tract	Social rank	Urbani- zation	Segrega- tion	Census tract	Social rank	Urbani- zation	Segrega- tion
9	28	23	9	289	22	25	8
10	28	21	11	325	29	33	9
68	25	40	10	336-B	18	27	9
268	28	45	6	349	23	38	0
269	23	36	6	352	27	25	4
271	26	37	4	354-B	17	18	0
272	28	42	6	488	25	31	12
273	28	39	7	503	27	44	2
275	28	32	7	506	23	22	3
280	26	27	6	512	18	28	8
281	28	32	4	515	23	34	5
282	26	31	3	523	29	24	3
283	20	21	2	524	27	33	8
284	27	26	4	549	29	34	12

High Index of Segregation

Census tract	Social rank	Urbani- zation	Segrega- tion	Census tract	Social rank	Urbani- zation	Segrega- tion
4	20	17	35	119	8	27	83
8	27	27	23	120	9	38	61
67	13	29	70	121	7	38	85
73	26	41	17	122	15	46	64
118	10	40	90	124	20	35	46

APPENDIX B—*Continued*

Area II: High Index of Segregation—*Continued*

Census tract	Social rank	Urbani-zation	Segrega-tion	Census tract	Social rank	Urbani-zation	Segrega-tion
125	19	47	68	335	28	23	39
126	25	51	36	338	23	31	43
127	25	49	46	340-A	23	34	50
130	22	35	67	364	13	23	100
131	23	49	48	448	22	22	60
132	20	36	47	450	29	38	15
133	23	34	38	456	25	32	29
134	25	36	14	458	22	28	46
143	25	35	30	484	23	37	45
224	25	47	92	485	17	30	66
247	26	51	37	486	15	35	68
253	22	36	83	487	21	29	34
255	29	36	90	489	23	30	15
285	20	23	34	490	3	18	87
286	20	22	90	491	3	14	79
287	11	14	84	499	20	20	34
292	16	30	39	501	11	26	78
293	23	50	34	502	14	42	80
295	29	30	22	513	26	32	16
296	17	42	31	518	22	23	18
297	25	38	18	539	15	21	27
299	29	48	16				

AREA III

Low social rank. High index of urbanization

Low Index of Segregation
No census tracts

High Index of Segregation

72	25	53	26	189	25	54	82
116	17	53	98	223	20	58	77
187	25	69	28	294	10	65	75
188	20	63	49	363	21	50	83

AREA IV

Middle social rank. Low index of urbanization

Low Index of Segregation

11	39	25	2	328	59	34	1
16	30	18	4	330	34	22	2
230	50	22	5	332-D	48	10	0

APPENDIX B—*Continued*

Area IV: Low Index of Segregation—*Continued*

Census tract	Social rank	Urbani-zation	Segrega-tion	Census tract	Social rank	Urbani-zation	Segrega-tion
350-A	36	23	2	470	57	27	3
351-A	38	24	3	532	36	23	0
392	44	24	3	534	40	20	2
397	54	31	1	535	31	12	3
434-A	59	30	1	547	47	27	13
440	56	31	2	559	38	12	1
464	40	22	6	560	39	14	6
465	44	23	11	561	47	27	6
467	32	19	13	563-A	37	17	6
468	37	20	3	565	51	25	4
469	39	23	2				

High Index of Segregation

353	33	18	17	542	38	21	26
446	57	33	35	543	35	22	45
447	41	25	44	548	34	22	29
471	47	27	24	558	36	16	16
541	57	26	16	564	35	18	15

AREA V

Middle social rank. Average index of urbanization

Low Index of Segregation

3	36	32	9	34	52	40	1
6	38	33	11	35	46	37	1
7	36	27	5	36	42	33	3
12	40	28	3	37	33	30	6
13	35	25	11	38	32	40	7
15	33	28	7	39	31	36	9
17	40	29	11	40	43	46	2
18	44	29	2	41	41	36	2
19	30	22	8	42	40	36	3
20	54	33	2	43	44	46	2
21	50	32	2	44	43	37	1
22	33	29	13	45	42	44	2
23	56	41	1	46	44	58	2
26	39	28	11	47	39	38	2
27	41	37	3	59	48	59	8
28	53	39	5	60	43	35	5
29	55	33	2	61	38	35	3
31	53	40	9	62	56	61	7

APPENDIX B—*Continued*

Area V: Low Index of Segregation—*Continued*

Census tract	Social rank	Urbanization	Segregation	Census tract	Social rank	Urbanization	Segregation
63	48	53	6	241	41	50	5
64	44	51	5	242	37	49	6
65	32	29	9	257	36	36	4
66	42	56	7	258	35	47	4
70	35	44	6	259	48	40	2
74	40	35	13	260	39	42	3
75	40	30	3	261	36	48	4
77	59	57	5	262	50	37	2
78	57	61	4	263	43	38	3
136	36	27	5	264	37	48	3
137	41	30	2	265	51	34	2
141	38	43	6	266	48	44	2
144	42	29	3	267	38	48	3
146	50	37	2	270	30	44	5
147	39	44	2	274	30	39	4
156	51	53	4	276	48	31	2
157	55	54	4	277	33	32	3
158	44	39	6	278	42	36	2
159	46	55	7	279	31	34	6
190	38	27	2	291	34	38	2
191	32	32	9	298	40	43	5
192	36	54	12	300	36	31	4
193	36	34	3	301	54	38	4
194	45	42	4	303	30	45	11
197	38	35	5	307	45	59	2
198	38	33	7	313	49	59	1
200	45	56	12	314	42	48	3
201	59	66	6	315	47	49	2
202	36	40	10	316	52	49	1
206	47	54	5	320	55	46	0
212	47	45	6	321	54	41	3
217	48	57	3	322	39	31	9
228	50	46	2	323	33	38	2
229	51	39	2	324	37	44	2
231	52	49	2	326	40	42	3
232	43	37	2	327	48	38	5
233	45	33	2	329	38	29	2
234	50	47	3	334	34	37	2
237	47	55	2	336-A	34	23	5
238	44	54	4	339	34	33	11
240	42	52	2	342-A	42	31	5

APPENDIX B—*Continued*

AREA V: Low Index of Segregation—*Continued*

Census tract	Social rank	Urbani- zation	Segrega- tion	Census tract	Social rank	Urbani- zation	Segrega- tion
342-B	49	31	0	443	53	33	6
343	42	35	2	444	51	38	1
345	56	34	5	453	59	43	11
346	42	39	1	454	51	43	1
347	38	26	1	455	31	36	3
348	37	29	4	457	44	41	12
350-B	31	28	1	460	56	36	8
357	39	38	5	461	40	47	0
359	45	40	6	474	58	48	3
360	53	34	2	476	55	46	2
362	34	25	1	477	51	37	4
367	46	41	2	478	43	38	4
368	39	40	5	479	50	46	3
372	37	51	7	480	52	36	2
375	38	55	11	481	40	31	2
378	51	50	2	482	34	29	3
386	51	48	6	483	35	31	7
390	50	33	2	492	31	34	5
391	39	38	5	493	40	40	5
393	54	33	1	494	53	39	4
394	38	49	10	495	53	40	2
398-A	41	33	3	496	47	37	4
400	51	37	1	504	32	35	1
401	51	56	2	505	33	34	2
402	46	55	3	507	33	31	1
403	43	55	12	508	41	33	3
404	54	48	2	509	48	57	2
405	52	51	2	510	30	50	7
407	50	61	2	514	31	41	4
412	53	46	1	516	32	30	6
413	47	41	2	521	43	35	1
414	36	33	9	522	31	31	1
418	47	43	6	526	36	29	2
419	50	41	2	530	32	33	8
422-A	46	34	2	531	43	32	2
422-B	49	42	1	537	40	27	4
423	47	50	4	544	40	29	9
425	32	50	13	545	52	48	1
430	59	43	2	546	39	37	1
431	50	35	2	550	32	28	9
442	52	31	7	551	42	30	10

APPENDIX B—*Continued*

AREA V: Low Index of Segregation—*Continued*

Census tract	Social rank	Urbani- zation	Segrega- tion	Census tract	Social rank	Urbani- zation	Segrega- tion
555	42	30	4	562	41	26	8
557	58	41	5	563-B	45	36	0

HIGH INDEX OF SEGREGATION

Census tract	Social rank	Urbani- zation	Segrega- tion	Census tract	Social rank	Urbani- zation	Segrega- tion
1	36	38	28	288	34	27	16
2	31	24	15	290	30	43	15
69	30	45	30	331	38	31	20
71	32	41	20	337-A	50	34	27
97	40	55	40	340-B	32	28	22
115	33	55	42	341-A	33	28	20
123	35	51	32	341-B	30	27	16
129	30	42	62	373	40	52	14
135	30	46	41	374	39	34	21
142	33	38	14	377	34	41	18
196	30	23	14	417	35	42	64
199	46	52	15	421	41	28	20
204	49	58	67	427	48	50	42
205	40	43	43	445	30	30	29
214	43	52	91	459	39	32	20
215	40	56	46	463	52	35	18
227	31	52	85	466	35	31	27
248	37	57	77	497	32	32	17
250	37	55	52	517	30	31	37
251	33	52	51	528	38	28	33
252	43	57	96	540	36	25	27
254	38	57	94	556	30	34	50
256	31	42	85				

AREA VI

Middle social rank. High index of urbanization

LOW INDEX OF SEGREGATION

54	57	75	8	104	52	67	5
83	57	77	9	105	44	65	12
84	52	73	7	108	51	85	10
85	53	70	6	110	58	91	4
88	41	59	6	111	57	96	2
89	53	75	5	112	53	93	4
90	55	66	5	114	47	66	10
92	56	72	4	162	56	72	3
103	53	77	7	168	59	75	4

APPENDIX B—*Continued*

AREA VI: Low Index of Segregation—*Continued*

Census tract	Social rank	Urbani- zation	Segrega- tion	Census tract	Social rank	Urbani- zation	Segrega- tion
169	46	65	6	218	50	67	4
170	53	92	3	220	35	89	13
171	43	69	8	235	49	63	4
172	54	87	5	236	47	72	6
173	46	90	4	239	41	62	7
174	51	85	3	243	43	75	8
175	39	78	3	244	38	66	10
176	49	85	5	245	36	61	9
177	36	74	6	246	32	55	8
178	46	84	5	304	45	67	7
179	37	75	9	305	46	64	3
181	41	82	9	306	48	67	4
182	48	88	5	308	46	63	1
183	53	84	4	309	47	68	2
184	39	93	9	310	49	78	1
203	59	67	10	311	56	75	2
208	55	67	6	376	57	71	1
210	38	67	13	380	45	79	6
211	50	68	8	406	50	69	2
213	45	65	12	424	52	70	2
216	48	69	11	511	41	59	2

HIGH INDEX OF SEGREGATION

Census tract	Social rank	Urbani- zation	Segrega- tion	Census tract	Social rank	Urbani- zation	Segrega- tion
81	54	71	17	185	40	88	17
87	48	69	16	186	32	87	36
106	57	71	22	209	43	67	20
107	53	75	16	219	46	73	14
113	34	57	35	221	33	71	19
117	40	69	66	222	36	69	18
128	32	62	42	225	30	56	79
166	51	70	24	226	32	57	96
167	42	62	26	249	37	58	69
180	33	70	26				

AREA VII

High social rank. Low index of urbanization

LOW INDEX OF SEGREGATION

Census tract	Social rank	Urbani- zation	Segrega- tion	Census tract	Social rank	Urbani- zation	Segrega- tion
50	86	45	5	365	84	37	3
332-A	65	30	7	395	71	26	0
332-C	70	30	1	409	69	35	1

APPENDIX B—*Continued*

Area VII: Low Index of Segregation—*Continued*

Census tract	Social rank	Urbani- zation	Segrega- tion	Census tract	Social rank	Urbani- zation	Segrega- tion
420	62	34	1	452	70	37	12
426	73	40	3	462-A	78	40	8
435	70	37	2	462-B	68	35	1
436	89	38	2	472	83	38	3
437	70	33	1	520	67	35	1
438-A	64	34	7	553	83	35	6
438-B	100	45	0	554-A	62	31	3
439	84	36	2	568	62	31	11
441	65	28	2				

HIGH INDEX OF SEGREGATION

Census tract	Social rank	Urbani- zation	Segrega- tion	Census tract	Social rank	Urbani- zation	Segrega- tion
337-B	86	36	20	356	69	35	17

AREA VIII

High social rank. Average index of urbanization

LOW INDEX OF SEGREGATION

Census tract	Social rank	Urbani- zation	Segrega- tion	Census tract	Social rank	Urbani- zation	Segrega- tion
24	63	36	3	149	69	68	5
25	62	39	3	150	71	65	5
30	77	64	5	151	66	59	7
32	65	49	7	152	66	56	5
33	62	37	1	153	60	57	4
48	82	46	7	154	61	67	6
49	68	42	5	155	62	49	5
51	77	48	6	160	73	57	5
52	72	63	6	163	68	64	7
57	66	62	4	195	68	39	3
58	67	69	5	207	62	54	4
76	62	55	5	312	63	68	1
79	69	66	6	317	64	52	1
82	75	68	8	318	65	55	1
91	62	65	4	319	65	45	2
93	78	62	4	361	61	54	1
94	62	67	4	379	67	48	2
98	80	51	7	381	91	53	4
99	74	73	5	382	76	64	3
138	83	54	4	383	70	67	3
139	65	42	1	385	68	60	3
140	60	39	4	387	74	64	6
145	68	43	3	399	64	40	1
148	70	63	6	408	67	38	1

APPENDIX B—*Continued*

AREA VIII: Low Index of Segregation—*Continued*

Census tract	Social rank	Urbanization	Segregation	Census tract	Social rank	Urbanization	Segregation
410	60	50	1	449	61	38	4
411	63	48	1	451	61	41	8
415	74	46	3	473	61	49	4
416	71	48	11	475	66	50	2
429	63	56	3	519	64	42	1
432	69	48	13	552	72	42	2
433	70	51	9	566	70	43	6

HIGH INDEX OF SEGREGATION

Census tract	Social rank	Urbanization	Segregation
567	64	51	19

AREA IX

High social rank. High index of urbanization

LOW INDEX OF SEGREGATION

Census tract	Social rank	Urbanization	Segregation	Census tract	Social rank	Urbanization	Segregation
53	67	80	4	101	71	94	5
55	69	81	4	102	66	80	4
56	61	74	7	109	70	89	4
80	71	80	8	161	63	73	4
86	60	82	5	164	76	84	5
95	61	68	4	165	68	90	5
96	63	83	3	428	61	73	4
100	71	78	3				

HIGH INDEX OF SEGREGATION

No census tracts.

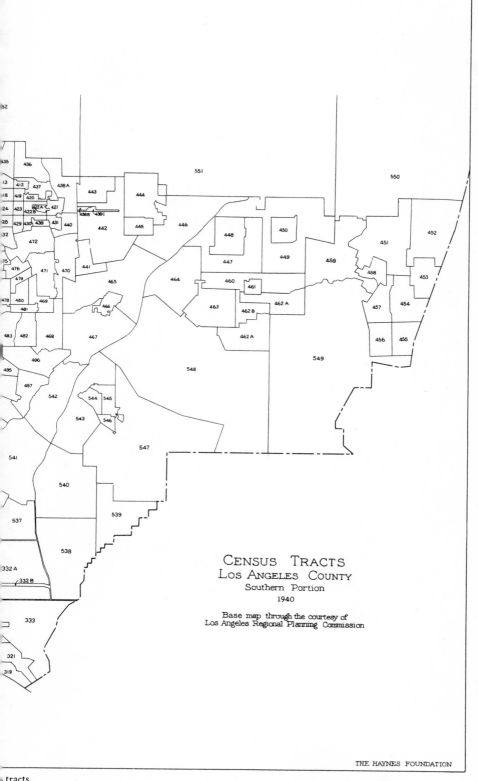

CENSUS TRACTS
LOS ANGELES COUNTY
Southern Portion
1940

Base map through the courtesy of
Los Angeles Regional Planning Commission

THE HAYNES FOUNDATION

tracts.

Fig. 63. Map of cens

APPENDIX C

APPENDIX C—*Continued*

Key to map	Name	Key to map	Name
81	Mount Washington	121	Santa Monica—South
82	Atwater	122	Santa Monica—Ocean Park
83	Silver Lake	123	Venice
84	Elysian Park	124	Del Rey
85	Chavez Ravine	125	Playa Del Rey
86	Echo Park	126	Westchester
87	Temple Street	127	Inglewood—West
88	Wholesale	128	View Park, Baldwin Hills
89	Bunker Hill	129	Leimert
90	Westlake	130	Inglewood—Hollywood Park
91	Downtown	131	South Vermont
92	Little Tokyo	132	Exposition Park
93	Figueroa-Adams	133	Central Avenue
94	West Jefferson	134	Green Meadows
95	West Adams Heights	135	Firestone Park
96	Berkeley Square	136	Watts
97	West Adams	137	South Gate
98	Pico-Vermont	138	Bell Gardens
99	Wilshire	139	Walnut Park
100	Beverly-Melrose, Vermont-Hoover	140	Huntington Park
		141	Bell
101	Hollywood—Southeast	142	Maywood
102	Hollywood Hills	143	Vernon
103	Hollywood—Central	144	Bandini
104	Hollywood—Southwest	145	Belvedere Gardens
105	West Hollywood	146	Belvedere Gardens—East
106	Beverly-Fairfax	147	Montebello—North
107	West Wilshire	148	Montebello—South
108	Wilshire-Pico	149	Pico, Rivera
109	Beverly Hills	150	Whittier
110	Westwood	151	Los Nietos
111	Cheviot Hills	152	Santa Fe Springs
112	Palms	153	Norwalk
113	Culver City	154	Artesia
114	Mar Vista	155	Lakewood Village, Mayfair
115	Sawtelle	156	Bellflower
116	West Los Angeles	157	Downey
117	Sawtelle-Government Reservation	158	Hynes, Clearwater
		159	Lynwood Gardens
118	Westgate	160	North Long Beach
119	Santa Monica—North	161	Compton
120	Santa Monica—Central	162	Lynwood

APPENDIX C—*Continued*

Key to map	Name	Key to map	Name
163	Willowbrook	176	San Pedro—Residential
164	Dominguez	177	Terminal Island
165	Torrance	178	Wilmington
166	Gardena	179	Long Beach—Central
167	Hawthorne	180	Long Beach—Belmont Heights
168	El Segundo	181	Long Beach—Commercial and Residential
169	Manhattan Beach		
170	Hermosa Beach	182	Signal Hill
171	Redondo Beach	183	Long Beach–California Heights–Bixby Knolls
172	Palos Verdes Estates		
173	Rolling Hills	184	Long Beach—East
174	San Pedro—Industrial	185	Avalon
175	San Pedro—Commercial		

APPENDIX D

185 NAMED PLACES

Key to map	Name	Census tracts	Social area
71	Alhambra	476–480	V
38	Altadena	434-A, 435–437, 438-A	VII
46	Arcadia	442	V
154	Artesia	538	I S
82	Atwater	60–61	V
185	Avalon	567	VIII S
51	Azusa	448	II S
78	Bairdstown, El Sereno	74–75, 136–137	V
64	Baldwin Park	464	IV
144	Bandini	498	I S
141	Bell	505, 507	V
156	Bellflower	537	V
138	Bell Gardens	506	II
75	Belvedere	485–486, 490–491	II S
145	Belvedere Gardens	487–489	II S
146	Belvedere Gardens—East	492–495	V
96	Berkeley Square	203	VI
19	Beverly Crest	49–50	VIII
106	Beverly-Fairfax	81	VI S
109	Beverly Hills	381–383	VIII
100	Beverly-Melrose, Vermont-Hoover	97	V S
76	Boyle Heights	121–135	II S
89	Bunker Hill	180–181	VI S
29	Burbank	390–394	V
13	Calabasas	565	IV
9	Canoga Park	14	I S
8	Canoga Park—Environs	13, 15	V
133	Central Avenue	223–227, 247–256	V S
5	Chatsworth	2	V S
85	Chavez Ravine	67	II S
111	Cheviot Hills	145	VIII
77	City Terrace	484	II S
57	Claremont	451–453	V
161	Compton	530–532, 534	V
53	Covina	460–461	V
113	Culver City	368	V
124	Del Rey	196, 363–364	V S
164	Dominguez	335	II S
157	Downey	541	IV S
91	Downtown	117, 173, 175, 177, 182–185	VI
50	Duarte	446	IV S

APPENDIX D—*Continued*

Key to map	Name	Census tracts	Social area
34	Eagle Rock	34-35	V
33	Eagle Rock—Hill Drive	33	VIII
86	Echo Park	105, 114	VI
65	El Monte	466	V S
168	El Segundo	362	V
84	Elysian Park	64, 66	V
17	Encino	28	V
132	Exposition Park	218, 235–236, 239, 243–246	VI
93	Figueroa-Adams	178–179, 219–222	VI S
135	Firestone Park	512–516, 518	II
27	Flintridge	553	VII
166	Gardena	288, 340-A–C, 341-A, B, 342-A, 343	V S
73	Garvey	467–468	IV
32	Glendale—Central	406	VI
28	Glendale—North	399, 408–411	VIII
31	Glendale—South	395, 397–398-A, 400–405, 407	V
54	Glendora	450	II S
4	Granada Hills	3	V
134	Green Meadows	268–275, 277–284	II
30	Griffith Park	31	V
167	Hawthorne	350-A, 351-A, 352, 353, 354-A–C, 358	I
170	Hermosa Beach	359	V
80	Highland Park	36, 40–47	V
103	Hollywood—Central	53–56	IX
102	Hollywood Hills	30, 52, 58	VIII
101	Hollywood—Southeast	85–86, 90–91, 95–96	IX
104	Hollywood—Southwest	78, 83–84, 88–89, 94	VI
140	Huntington Park	508–511	V
158	Hynes, Clearwater	536	I
130	Inglewood—Hollywood Park	345	V
127	Inglewood—West	346–348, 350-B	V
52	Irwindale	447	IV S
155	Lakewood Village, Mayfair	332-A	VII
45	Lamanda Park	440	IV
56	La Verne	458	II S
129	Leimert	207, 228–229, 231–233	V
79	Lincoln Heights	65, 68–73, 120	II S
92	Little Tokyo	186–189	III S
180	Long Beach—Belmont Heights	312, 317–319	VIII

APPENDIX D—*Continued*

Key to map	Name	Census tracts	Social area
183	Long Beach–California Heights– Bixby Knolls	328, 332-c	VII
179	Long Beach—Central	304–311	VI
181	Long Beach—Commercial and Residential	303, 313–316, 320–327	VI
184	Long Beach—East	333	I S
151	Los Nietos	543	IV S
162	Lynwood	526	V
159	Lynwood Gardens	535	IV
14	Malibu La Costa	566	VIII
169	Manhattan Beach	360	V
114	Mar Vista	144	V
142	Maywood	503–504	II
48	Monrovia—North	444	V
49	Monrovia—South	445	V S
147	Montebello—North	496	V
148	Montebello—South	497	V S
74	Monterey Park	481–483	V
26	Montrose	554-A	VII
81	Mount Washington	37–39	V
21	North Hollywood	20–24	V
160	North Long Beach	329–330	IV
6	Northridge	8	II S
153	Norwalk	539–540	V S
15	Pacific Palisades, Brentwood, Bel-Air	48	VIII
3	Pacoima	4	II S
112	Palms	146–147, 367	V
172	Palos Verdes Estates	337-B	VII S
35	Pasadena—Annandale	426	VII
40	Pasadena—Central	424, 428	IX
39	Pasadena—Commercial and Residential	412–413, 418–419, 422-A, B, 423, 430–431	V
43	Pasadena—East Colorado	421	V S
42	Pasadena—East Orange Grove	420	VII
37	Pasadena—Lincoln Avenue	414, 417, 425, 427	V S
36	Pasadena—Linda Vista	415–416	VIII
41	Pasadena—Oak Knoll	429, 432–433	VIII
149	Pico, Rivera	542	IV S
98	Pico-Vermont	162, 166–171	VI S
125	Playa Del Rey	195	VIII
58	Pomona—North and Southeast	454–455, 457	V
59	Pomona—Southwest	456	II S

APPENDIX D—*Continued*

Key to map	Name	Census tracts	Social area
61	Puente	548	IV S
171	Redondo Beach	357	V
10	Reseda	16	IV
173	Rolling Hills	337-A	V S
22	Roscoe	5, 10, 19	I
66	Rosemead	465	IV
55	San Dimas	459	V S
2	San Fernando	556	V S
68	San Gabriel	471	IV S
69	San Marino	439, 472	VII
175	San Pedro—Commercial	298, 300	V
174	San Pedro—Industrial	295–297, 299, 331	II S
176	San Pedro—Residential	301	V
44	Santa Anita Oaks	438-B	VII
152	Santa Fe Springs	547	IV
120	Santa Monica—Central	376	VI
119	Santa Monica—North	378–379	VIII
122	Santa Monica—Ocean Park	372	V
121	Santa Monica—South	373–375, 377	V S
115	Sawtelle	143	II S
117	Sawtelle–Government Reservation	380	VI
7	Sepulveda	9	II
18	Sherman Oaks	29	V
47	Sierra Madre	443	V
182	Signal Hill	334	V
83	Silver Lake	32, 59, 62–63, 87, 92, 103–104	V
137	South Gate	521–524	V
70	South Pasadena	473–475	VIII
131	South Vermont	206, 217, 234, 237–238, 240–242, 257–267, 276, 342-B	V
20	Studio City	25	VIII
24	Sunland	6–7	V
1	Sylmar	1	V S
16	Tarzana	27	V
67	Temple City	441, 470	IV
87	Temple Street	113, 115	V S
177	Terminal Island	294	III S
165	Torrance	289, 336-A, B, 338–339, 355	II
25	Tujunga	12, 555	V
11	Van Nuys	17–18	V
123	Venice	190–194	V
23	Verdugo Hills	11	IV

APPENDIX D—*Continued*

Key to map	Name	Census tracts	Social area
143	Vernon	499, 501	II S
128	View Park, Baldwin Hills	365	VII
139	Walnut Park	519–520	VIII
60	Walnut, Spadra	549	II
136	Watts	285–287, 517	II S
97	West Adams	156–159, 197–202	V S
95	West Adams Heights	208	VI
126	Westchester	230	IV
62	West Covina—East	462-B	VII
63	West Covina—West	463	V S
118	Westgate	140	VIII
103	West Hollywood	51, 57, 76–77, 385–387	VIII
94	West Jefferson	204–205, 209–216	V S
90	Westlake	106–108, 110–112, 172, 174, 176	VI S
116	West Los Angeles	141–142	V S
107	West Wilshire	79–80, 82	IX
110	Westwood	138–139	VIII
150	Whittier	544–546	V
88	Wholesale	116, 118–119	II S
163	Willowbrook	527–529	I S
72	Wilmar	469	IV
178	Wilmington	290–293	II S
99	Wilshire	93, 98–102, 109, 160–161, 163–165	IX
108	Wilshire-Pico	148–155	VIII
12	Woodland Hills	26	V

CENSUS TRACTS WITH POPULATIONS TOO SMALL OR TOO SCATTERED FOR INCLUSION IN 185 NAMED PLACES

Identifying place name	Census tract	Social area
Covina Suburbs	462-A	VII
El Porto Beach	361	VIII
Glendora Suburbs	449	VIII
Inglewood	349	II
Long Beach	332-D	V
Redondo Beach	356	VII S
Vernon	502	II S

APPENDIX E

AREA I
Low social rank. Low index of urbanization

LOW INDEX OF SEGREGATION

Key to map	Name	Key to map	Name
167	Hawthorne	22	Roscoe
158	Hynes, Clearwater		

HIGH INDEX OF SEGREGATION

Key to map	Name	Key to map	Name
154	Artesia	184	Long Beach—East
144	Bandini	163	Willowbrook
9	Canoga Park		

AREA II
Low social rank. Average index of urbanization
LOW INDEX OF SEGREGATION

Key to map	Name	Key to map	Name
138	Bell Gardens	7	Sepulveda
135	Firestone Park	165	Torrance
134	Green Meadows	60	Walnut, Spadra
142	Maywood		

HIGH INDEX OF SEGREGATION

Key to map	Name	Key to map	Name
51	Azusa	6	Northridge
75	Belvedere	3	Pacoima
145	Belvedere Gardens	59	Pomona—Southwest
76	Boyle Heights	174	San Pedro—Industrial
85	Chavez Ravine	115	Sawtelle
77	City Terrace	143	Vernon
164	Dominguez	136	Watts
54	Glendora	88	Wholesale
56	La Verne	178	Wilmington
79	Lincoln Heights		

AREA III
Low social rank. High index of urbanization

LOW INDEX OF SEGREGATION
No named places.

HIGH INDEX OF SEGREGATION

Key to map	Name	Key to map	Name
92	Little Tokyo	177	Terminal Island

APPENDIX E—*Continued*

AREA IV

Middle social rank. Low index of urbanization

LOW INDEX OF SEGREGATION

Key to map	Name	Key to map	Name
64	Baldwin Park	66	Rosemead
13	Calabasas	152	Santa Fe Springs
73	Garvey	67	Temple City
45	Lamanda Park	23	Verdugo Hills
159	Lynwood Gardens	126	Westchester
160	North Long Beach	72	Wilmar
10	Reseda		

HIGH INDEX OF SEGREGATION

157	Downey	149	Pico, Rivera
50	Duarte	61	Puente
52	Irwindale	68	San Gabriel
151	Los Nietos		

AREA V

Middle social rank. Average index of urbanization

LOW INDEX OF SEGREGATION

71	Alhambra	170	Hermosa Beach
46	Arcadia	80	Highland Park
82	Atwater	140	Huntington Park
78	Bairdstown, El Sereno	130	Inglewood—Hollywood Park
141	Bell	127	Inglewood—West
156	Bellflower	129	Leimert
146	Belvedere Gardens—East	162	Lynwood
29	Burbank	169	Manhattan Beach
8	Canoga Park—Environs	114	Mar Vista
57	Claremont	48	Monrovia—North
161	Compton	147	Montebello—North
53	Covina	74	Monterey Park
113	Culver City	81	Mount Washington
34	Eagle Rock	21	North Hollywood
168	El Segundo	112	Palms
84	Elysian Park	39	Pasadena—Commercial and Residential
17	Encino		
31	Glendale—South	58	Pomona—North and Southeast
4	Granada Hills	171	Redondo Beach
30	Griffith Park	175	San Pedro—Commercial

APPENDIX E—*Continued*

AREA V: Low Index of Segregation—*Continued*

Key to map	Name	Key to map	Name
176	San Pedro—Residential	24	Sunland
122	Santa Monica—Ocean Park	16	Tarzana
18	Sherman Oaks	25	Tujunga
47	Sierra Madre	11	Van Nuys
182	Signal Hill	123	Venice
83	Silver Lake	150	Whittier
137	South Gate	12	Woodland Hills
131	South Vermont		

HIGH INDEX OF SEGREGATION

Key to map	Name	Key to map	Name
100	Beverly-Melrose, Vermont-Hoover	37	Pasadena—Lincoln Avenue
133	Central Avenue	173	Rolling Hills
5	Chatsworth	55	San Dimas
124	Del Rey	2	San Fernando
65	El Monte	121	Santa Monica—South
166	Gardena	1	Sylmar
49	Monrovia—South	87	Temple Street
148	Montebello—South	97	West Adams
153	Norwalk	63	West Covina—West
43	Pasadena—East Colorado	94	West Jefferson
		116	West Los Angeles

AREA VI

Middle social rank. High index of urbanization

LOW INDEX OF SEGREGATION

Key to map	Name	Key to map	Name
96	Berkeley Square	181	Long Beach—Commercial and Residential
91	Downtown		
86	Echo Park	120	Santa Monica—Central
132	Exposition Park	117	Sawtelle—Government Reservation
32	Glendale–Central		
104	Hollywood—Southwest	95	West Adams Heights
179	Long Beach—Central		

HIGH INDEX OF SEGREGATION

Key to map	Name	Key to map	Name
106	Beverly-Fairfax	98	Pico-Vermont
89	Bunker Hill	90	Westlake
93	Figueroa-Adams		

APPENDIX E—*Continued*

AREA VII

High social rank. Low index of urbanization

LOW INDEX OF SEGREGATION

Key to map	Name	Key to map	Name
38	Altadena	35	Pasadena—Annandale
27	Flintridge	42	Pasadena—East Orange Grove
155	Lakewood Village, Mayfair	69	San Marino
183	Long Beach–California Heights–Bixby Knolls	44	Santa Anita Oaks
		128	View Park, Baldwin Hills
26	Montrose	62	West Covina—East

HIGH INDEX OF SEGREGATION

172   Palos Verdes Estates

AREA VIII

High social rank. Average index of urbanization

LOW INDEX OF SEGREGATION

19	Beverly Crest	41	Pasadena—Oak Knoll
109	Beverly Hills	125	Playa Del Rey
111	Cheviot Hills	119	Santa Monica—North
33	Eagle Rock—Hill Drive	70	South Pasadena
28	Glendale—North	20	Studio City
102	Hollywood Hills	139	Walnut Park
180	Long Beach—Belmont Heights	118	Westgate
14	Malibu La Costa	105	West Hollywood
15	Pacific Palisades, Brentwood, Bel-Air	110	Westwood
36	Pasadena—Linda Vista	108	Wilshire-Pico

HIGH INDEX OF SEGREGATION

185   Avalon

AREA IX

High social rank. High index of urbanization

LOW INDEX OF SEGREGATION

103	Hollywood—Central	107	West Wilshire
101	Hollywood—Southeast	99	Wilshire
40	Pasadena—Central		

HIGH INDEX OF SEGREGATION

No named places.

APPENDIX F

MUNICIPALITIES: ALPHABETICAL LIST, WITH INDEXES OF SOCIAL RANK,
URBANIZATION, SEGREGATION, AND SOCIAL-AREA NUMBER

Municipality	Social rank	Urbanization	Segregation	Social area
Alhambra	51	40	3	V
Arcadia	52	31	7	V
Avalon	64	51	19	VIII S
Azusa	22	22	60	II S
Bell	33	34	2	V
Beverly Hills	79	62	3	VIII
Burbank	45	33	4	V
Claremont	59	43	11	V
Compton	37	33	5	V
Covina	40	47	0	V
Culver City	39	40	5	V
El Monte	35	31	27	V S
El Segundo	34	25	1	V
Gardena City	31	28	20	V S
Glendale	55	46	2	V
Glendora	29	38	15	II S
Hawthorne	27	25	4	II
Hermosa Beach	45	40	6	V
Huntington Park	41	48	3	V
Inglewood	42	33	3	V
La Verne	22	28	46	II S
Long Beach	47	47	3	V
Lynwood	36	29	2	V
Manhattan Beach	53	34	2	V
Maywood	31	36	1	V
Monrovia	44	35	10	V
Montebello	39	34	11	V
Monterey Park	37	30	3	V
Palos Verdes Estates	86	36	20	VII S
Pasadena	51	48	10	V
Pomona	39	38	11	V
Redondo Beach	33	31	7	V
San Fernando	30	34	50	V S
San Gabriel	47	27	24	IV S
San Marino	83	38	3	VII
Santa Monica	48	48	9	V
Sierra Madre	53	33	6	V
Signal Hill	34	37	2	V
South Gate	35	31	2	V

APPENDIX F—*Continued*

Municipality	Social rank	Urbaniza- tion	Segrega- tion	Social area
South Pasadena..................	62	49	3	VIII
Torrance.......................	29	32	21	II S
Vernon.........................	11	26	78	II S
West Covina....................	56	35	14	V S
Whittier.......................	45	40	3	V

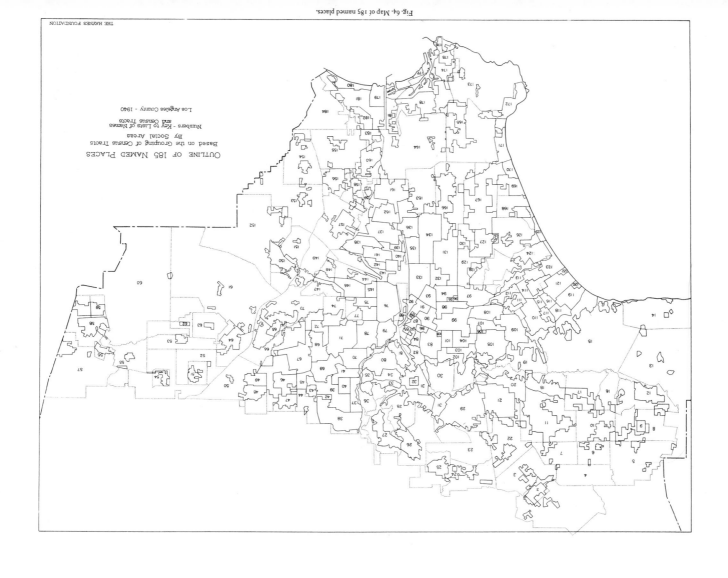

Fig. 64. Map of 185 named places.

OUTLINE OF 185 NAMED PLACES
Based on the Grouping of Census Tracts
By Social Areas
Numbers - Key to Lists of Names
and Census Tracts
Los Angeles County - 1940

NOTE ON 185 NAMED PLACES

SOME area larger than the census tract and smaller than the municipality is often needed for the convenient handling of census-tract data. The manner in which the census tracts are grouped to form these intermediate statistical areas depends on the purposes for which the statistics are to be used. The statistical areas of the Regional Planning Commission, the "16 major economic areas" and "105 census of business areas" developed for the study of the Los Angeles retail market, the planning areas of the Board of Education, the "communities" of Los Angeles as defined by the City Planning Commission, and the study areas of the Welfare Council of Metropolitan Los Angeles are all groupings of census tracts that facilitate over-all study and interpretation. The 185 named places presented here are not intended as alternative groups of census tracts to take the place of any others now in use for particular purposes, but were developed to fill our need in this study of areas containing adjacent census tracts in the same social area.

The 185 named places listed in Appendixes C, D, and E, and shown on the map herewith (fig. 64), are each composed of contiguous census tracts having approximately the same social characteristics as are measured by the criteria we have chosen. The numbers on the map correspond to those in the lists in Appendixes C, D, and E, and are given in each list opposite the identifying name. Census tracts included in each place are given in Appendix D, with the social area in which each is found. All the tracts in any given place are either in the same social area or border closely upon that area. The larger municipalities have been divided into as many sections as is necessary in order to maintain the homogeneity of each named place.

Together, the tracts comprising these 185 places include all tracts in the southern section of Los Angeles County, south of the San Gabriel Mountains, except those with a population of less than 50, for which no indexes were calculated, and other tracts where populations were either too small or too scattered for the purposes of this grouping. Identifying place names adopted are those of municipalities and of sections of municipalities, names of unincorporated places, and other neighborhood designations in general use. Throughout the text these same names are used as identifying place names when reference is made to any one census tract.

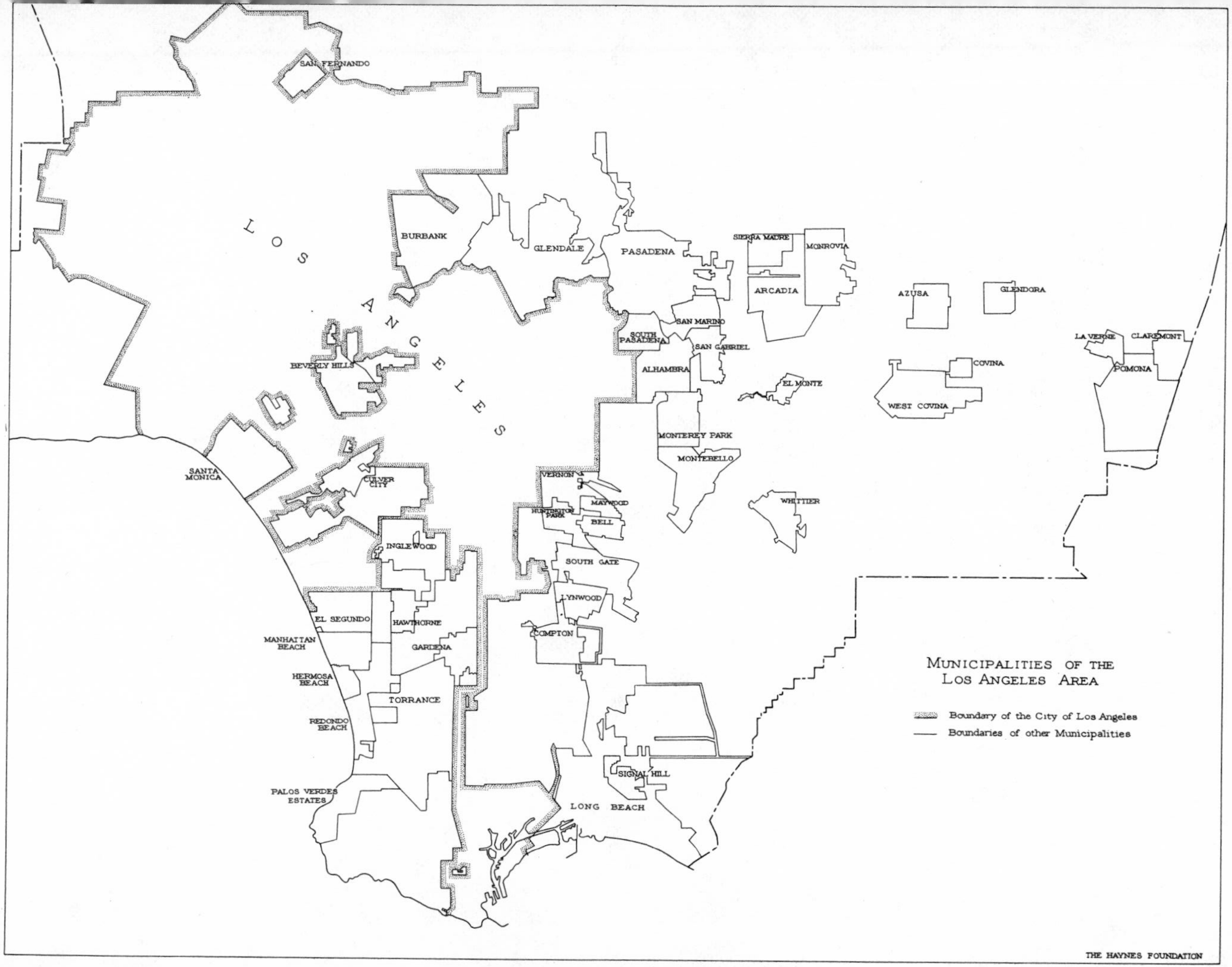

MUNICIPALITIES OF THE
LOS ANGELES AREA

— Boundary of the City of Los Angeles
— Boundaries of other Municipalities

THE HAYNES FOUNDATION

Fig. 65. Map showing the municipalities of Los Angeles County.

Bibliography

Bean, Louis H. "International Industrialization and Per Capita Income," *Studies in Income and Wealth*, Vol. 8, National Bureau of Economic Research, New York, 1946.

Caldwell, M. G. "The Adjustments of Mountain Families in an Urban Environment," *Social Forces*, 16 (1938), pp. 389–395.

Choun, H. F. "Dust Storms in the Southwestern Plains Area," *Monthly Weather Review*, 64 (1936), pp. 195–199.

Clark, Colin. *Conditions of Economic Progress*, London, 1940.

———. "The Economic Functions of a City in Relation to Its Size," *Econometrica*, 13 (1945), pp. 97–113.

Cohen, Morris R. *Reason and Nature: An Essay on the Meaning of Scientific Method*, New York, 1931.

Crum, W. L. "Regional Diversity of Income Distribution," *American Journal of Sociology*, 24 (1936), pp. 215–225.

Davis, Kingsley. "A Conceptual Analysis of Stratification," *American Sociological Review*, 7 (1942), pp. 309–321.

———. "The World Demographic Transition," *Annals of the American Academy of Political and Social Science*, 237 (1945), pp. 1–11.

Davis, Kingsley, and Wilbert E. Moore. "Some Principles of Stratification," *American Sociological Review*, 10 (1945), pp. 242–249.

Dublin, Louis I., and Alfred J. Lotka. *Length of Life*, New York, 1937.

Durand, John D. "Married Women in the Labor Force," *American Sociological Review*, 52 (1946), pp. 217–223.

Edwards, Alba M. "A Social-Economic Grouping of the Gainful Workers of the United States," *Journal of the American Statistical Association*, 28 (1933), pp. 377–387.

———. *A Social-Economic Grouping of the Gainful Workers of the United States, 1930*, Bureau of the Census, Washington, D.C., 1938.

Fei, Hsiao-T'ung, and Chih-I Chang. *Earthbound China: A Study of Rural Economy in Yunnan*, University of Chicago Press, Chicago, 1944.

Firey, Walter. *Land Use in Central Boston*, Harvard University Press, Cambridge, 1947.

Gerth, H. H., and C. Wright Mills, trans. and eds. *From Max Weber: Essays in Sociology*, Oxford University Press, New York, 1946.

Goldschmidt, Walter. *As You Sow*, New York, 1947.

Goodrich, Carter, and others. *Migration and Economic Opportunity*, Report of the Study of Population Redistribution, University of Pennsylvania Press, Philadelphia, 1936.

Hatt, Paul. "Spatial Patterns in a Polyethnic Area," *American Sociological Review*, 10 (1945), p. 355.

Heflin, Catherine P., and Howard W. Beers. "Urban Adjustments of Rural Migrants," Kentucky Agricultural Experiment Station, *Bulletin 487*, Lexington, 1946.

Henderson, L. J. *Pareto's General Sociology—A Physiologist's Interpretation*, Harvard University Press, Cambridge, 1935.

Hill, Joseph A. "Women in Gainful Occupations, 1870–1920," *Census Monograph IX*. Washington, D.C., 1929.

Hollingshead, August B. "Community Research: Development and Present Condition," *American Sociological Review*, 13 (1948), pp. 136–146.

Jaffe, A. J. "Differential Fertility in the White Population in Early America," *Journal of Heredity*, 31 (1940), pp. 407–411.

———. "Population Growth and Fertility Trends in the United States," *Journal of Heredity*, 32 (1941), pp. 441–445.

———. "Urbanization and Fertility," *American Journal of Sociology*, 48 (1942), pp. 48–60.

Jaffe, A. J., and Seymour L. Wolfbein. "Internal Migration and Full Employment in the United States," *Journal of the American Statistical Association*, 40 (1945), pp. 351–363.

Jahn, Julius, Calvin F. Schmid, and Clarence Schrag. "The Measurement of Ecological Segregation," *American Sociological Review*, 12 (1947), pp. 293–303.

Janow, Seymour J. "Volume and Characteristics of Recent Migration to the Far West," Committee on Interstate Migration of Destitute Citizens (Tolan Committee), *Hearings*, Washington, D.C., 1941, pp. 2299–2301.

Kirk, Dudley. *Europe's Population in the Interwar Years*, League of Nations Publications II, Economic and Financial, 1946, II A 8.

Kirk, Hazel. "Who Works and Why," *Annals of the American Academy of Political and Social Science*, 251 (1947), pp. 44–52.

Kluver, Heinrich. "The Problem of Types," *Journal of Philosophy*, 22 (1925), pp. 225–234.

Lang, Richard O. "Population Characteristics Associated with Educational Levels and Economic Status in Chicago," *American Sociological Review*, 2 (1937), pp. 187–194.

Lazarsfeld, Paul F. "Some Remarks on the Typological Procedures in Social Research," *Zeitschrift für Sozialforschung*, 6 (1937), pp. 119–139.

Leyburn, Grace. "Urban Adjustments of Migrants from the Southern Appalachian Plateau," *Social Forces*, 16 (1937), pp. 238–246.

Linton, Ralph. *The Study of Man*, New York, 1936.

Los Angeles County-wide Hospital Survey. *A Hospital Plan for Los Angeles County*, James A. Hamilton and Associates, Los Angeles, 1947.

Lynd, Robert S., and Helen M. Lynd. *Middletown*, New York, 1929.

———. *Middletown in Transition*, New York, 1937.

McKenzie, R. D. *The Metropolitan Community*, New York, 1933.

McWilliams, Carey. *Southern California Country*, New York, 1946.

Miller, Frieda S. "Women in the Labor Force," *Annals of the American Academy of Political and Social Science*, 251 (1947), pp. 35–43.

Moe, Edward O., and Carl C. Taylor. *Culture of a Contemporary Rural Community: Irwin, Iowa*, Rural Life Studies, No. 5, Bureau of Agricultural Economics, Washington, D.C., 1942.

Myers, Charles A., and W. Rupert MacLaurin. *The Movement of Factory Workers: A Study of a New England Industrial Community*, New York, 1943.

National Resources Committee. *Our Cities: Their Role in the National Economy*, Washington, D.C., 1937.

———. *The Problems of a Changing Population*, Washington, D.C., 1938.

New York State Commission of Housing and Regional Planning. *Final Report*, Albany, 1926.

Notestein, Frank W. "The Differential Rate of Increase Among the Social Classes of the American Population," *Social Forces*, 12 (1933), pp. 17–33.

———. "Class Differences in Fertility," *Annals of the American Academy of Political and Social Science*, 188 (1936), pp. 26–36.

Odum, Howard W. *Southern Regions of the United States*, Southern Regional Committee of the Social Science Research Council, Chapel Hill, 1936.

Park, R. E., and E. W. Burgess. *The City*, University of Chicago Press, Chicago, 1925.

Pearl, Raymond. "Some Aspects of the Biology of Human Populations," in E. V. Cowdry, *Human Biology and Racial Welfare*, New York, 1930, pp. 521–525.

———. "A Classification and Code of Occupations," *Human Biology*, 5 (1933), pp. 491–505.

———. "The Aging of Populations," *Journal of the American Statistical Association*, 35 (1940), pp. 277–297.

Population Committee for the Central Valley Project Studies. *Statistical Memorandum No. 6*, Berkeley, 1944, pp. 1–11.

Quetelet, Lambert Adolphe Jacques. *Du système social et des lois qui le régissent*, Paris, 1848.

Shils, Edward. *The Present State of American Sociology*, The Free Press, Glencoe, Ill., 1948.

Shryock, Henry S., Jr., and Hope Tisdale Eldridge. "Internal Migration in Peace and War," *American Sociological Review*, 12 (1947), pp. 27–39.

Smith, T. Lynn. "Some Aspects of Village Demography," *Social Forces*, 20 (1941), pp. 15–25.

———. *Brazil: People and Institutions*, Louisiana State University Press, Baton Rouge, 1946.

Speier, Hans. "Social Stratification in the Urban Community," *American Sociological Review*, 1 (1932), pp. 193–202.

Sundbärg, A. G. Institut International de Statistique, *Bulletin*, 12 (1900), pp. 90–95.

Thomas, Dorothy Swaine. "Research Memorandum on Migration Differentials," Social Science Research Council, *Bulletin 43*, New York, 1938.

Thompson, Warren S. "Ratio of Children to Women in the United States, 1920," *Census Monograph XI*, Washington, D.C., 1931.

———. *Average Number of Children per Woman in Butler County, Ohio: 1930—A Study in Differential Fertility*, Bureau of the Census, Washington, D.C., 1941.

———. *Population Problems*, New York, 1942.

Thornthwaite, C. W. *Internal Migration in the United States*, Philadelphia, 1934.

United States. Bureau of the Census. *Sixteenth Census of the United States, 1940,* "Population and Housing, Statistics for Census Tracts: Los Angeles–Long Beach, Calif.," Washington, D.C., 1942.

———. *Sixteenth Census of the United States, 1940,* "Population and Housing, Statistics for Census Tracts [for various cities]," Washington, D.C., 1942.

———. *Sixteenth Census of the United States, 1940,* "Population, Characteristics of the Population," Vol. 2, Washington, D.C., 1943.

———. *Sixteenth Census of the United States, 1940,* "Population, Differential Fertility, 1940 and 1910, Fertility for States and Larger Cities," Washington, D.C., 1943.

———. *Sixteenth Census of the United States, 1940,* "Population, Internal Migration, 1935 to 1940, Color and Sex of Migrants," Washington, D.C., 1943.

Vance, Rupert B. "Research Memorandum on Population Redistribution Within the United States," Social Science Research Council, *Bulletin 42,* New York, 1938.

———. *All These People,* Chapel Hill, 1946.

Warner, W. Lloyd, and Paul S. Lunt. *The Social Life of a Modern Community,* Yale University Press, New Haven, 1941.

Warner, W. Lloyd, and Leo Srole. *The Social Systems of American Ethnic Groups,* Yale University Press, New Haven, 1945.

Weber, Adna Ferrin. *The Growth of Cities in the Nineteenth Century—A Study in Statistics,* New York, 1899.

Weeks, David. *Permissible Economic Rate of Irrigation Development in California,* California Division of Water Resources, Bulletin No. 35, 1930.

Whelpton, P. K. "Occupational Groups in the United States, 1820–1920," *Journal of the American Statistical Association,* 21 (1926), pp. 335–343.

———. "Industrial Development and Population Growth," *Social Forces,* 6 (1928), pp. 458–467, 629–638.

———. "Geographic and Economic Differentials in Fertility," *Annals of the American Academy of Political and Social Science,* 188 (1936), pp. 37–55.

Wilcox, Walter F. "The Change in the Proportion of Children in the United States and in the Birth Rate in France during the Nineteenth Century," American Statistical Association, *Publications,* 12 (1910–1911), pp. 490–499.

———. *Studies in American Demography,* Cornell University Press, 1940.

Winch, Robert F. "Heuristic and Empirical Typologies: A Job for Factor Analysis," *American Sociological Review,* 12 (1947), pp. 68–75.

Wolfbein, S. L., and A. J. Jaffe. "Demographic Factors in Labor Force Growth," *American Sociological Review,* 11 (1946), pp. 392–396.

Index